Dollars & Sense
PATHWAY TO GENUINE PROSPERITY

ALAN JOHNSTON

Dollars & Sense

Copyright © 2023 by Alan Johnston

All rights reserved.

ISBN 979-8-88758-014-2 Paperback

ISBN 979-8-88758-015-9 Ebook

No part of this book may be reproduced in any form or by any electronic or mechanical means, including information storage and retrieval systems, without written permission from the author, except for the use of brief quotations in a book review.

Scripture quotations not otherwise marked are from the ESV® Bible (The Holy Bible, English Standard Version®), © 2001 by Crossway, a publishing ministry of Good News Publishers. Used by permission. All rights reserved. The ESV text may not be quoted in any publication made available to the public by a Creative Commons license. The ESV may not be translated in whole or in part into any other language.

Scripture quotations marked (NIV) are taken from the Holy Bible, New International Version®, NIV®. Copyright © 1973, 1978, 1984, 2011 by Biblica, Inc.™ Used by permission of Zondervan. All rights reserved worldwide. www.zondervan.com. The "NIV" and "New International Version" are trademarks registered in the United States Patent and Trademark Office by Biblica, Inc.™

Scripture quotations marked (CSB) have been taken from the Christian Standard Bible®, Copyright © 2017 by Holman Bible Publishers. Used by permission. Christian Standard Bible® and CSB® are federally registered trademarks of Holman Bible Publishers.

Scripture quotations marked (CEV) are from the Contemporary English Version Copyright © 1991, 1992, 1995 by American Bible Society, Used by Permission.

Scripture quotations marked (MSG) are taken from *THE MESSAGE*. Copyright © 1993, 1994, 1995, 1996, 2000, 2001, 2002. Used by permission of NavPress Publishing Group.

Published by Soncoast Publishing
P.O. Box 1504
Hartselle, AL 35640
www.soncoastpublishing.com

Contents

Dollars & Sense	v
Foreword	ix
1. The Promise: Peace and Prosperity	1
2. The Pathway: What is Financial Planning?	11
3. The Problem: Roadblocks to Financial Freedom	21
4. The Peril: The Danger of Debt	29
5. The Provision: God the Provider	41
6. The Psychology: Lessons from Behavioral Science	47
7. The Principles: Money and the Bible	55
8. The Process: Financial Planning Concepts	75
9. The Purchase: Colleges, Cars and Cottages	105
10. The Payment: Paying Less to Ceasar	113
11. The Plan: Has the Gold Tarnished in Your Retirement Plan?	119
12. The Passage: Where There's a Will, There's a Way	129
13. The Pleasure: God Loves a Cheerful Giver	137
14. The Perspective: Learning to Balance Life	153
15. The Preparation: Parents - Children - Widows	161
16. The Progress: Creating Accountability for Personal Success	173
Afterword	179
Dictionary Of Financial Planning Terms	181
Appendix	189
About the Author	191
Also by Alan Johnston	193

Dollars & Sense
PATHWAY TO GENUINE PROSPERITY

"...put God's work first and do what he wants. Then the other things will be yours as well." Matthew 6:33 (CEV)

"God wanted to make known among the Gentiles the glorious wealth of this mystery, which is Christ in you, the hope of glory. Colossians 1:27 (NIV)

"For I know the plans I have for you...plans for your well-being, not for disaster, to give you a hope and a future." Jeremiah 29:11 (CSB)

Dr. Alan Johnston, CFP®, ChFC, AEP

This book is dedicated to

*Pastor Hughie Denton
and
Geraldine, his dear, sweet wife*

Foreword

I will never forget my introduction to "financial planning." I was a young pastor with very limited resources, a young daughter, a college bill to pay and living expenses like those of any other person. About the only thing I had done toward planning at that point was to have purchased a life insurance policy, and the church was investing $34.00 per month in an annuity on my behalf. Beyond that, we basically lived from check to check. There was no plan for the present or the future. A pastor friend, Rev. Hughie Denton, who was visiting in our home, sat me down with a little ledger book and showed me the most fundamental aspects of planning one's finances. For the first time, I had a plan.

Financial planning has continued to evolve in my household to the point now where we have some rather extensive and comprehensive financial and estate plans. I have discovered that financial planning is never done; it is never complete. The planning process has to be as flexible as our circumstances and as broad as our concerns.

I prepared this book because first, I felt very strongly that it was God's instruction and direction which led me to do so. Furthermore, I am convinced that financial planning belongs in the vocabulary of the church and the Christian. In more than fifty-five years of ministry, combined with thirty-seven years of work as a financial planner, I have

FOREWORD

witnessed the repeated mistakes of too many Christians – who either out of neglect, lack of knowledge, or the lack of discipline – find themselves in a financial quagmire of their own making.

The community of faith cannot afford to ignore this topic which demanded so much attention from Jesus. The counselor's office is overflowing with believers who have not learned to be stewards (managers) of their God-provided resources.

I am indebted to many people who have contributed to my understanding of this subject. At the top of that list goes Pastor Hughie Denton. As a teenager, growing up at Mt. Hebron Baptist Church in Elmore, Alabama, nearby, in Millbrook, Alabama, Pastor Hughie was Pastor of the Millbrook Baptist Church. As an eighteen year old preacher, Hughie took me under his wing, and I am forever grateful for the wisdom he provided, and for the willingness he had to allow a "green-horn" teenage preacher stand in the pulpit and preach. As the years passed Hughie and his wonderful wife Geraldine hosted me in their home countless times. Geraldine's smile was infectious, and her laughter could make even an old curmudgeon smile. Through the years I was privileged to preach many revivals for Brother Hughie. I love to preach – and Hughie always made our revival times special. The best part was staying in the home of Geraldine and Hughie Denton. That history remains among my most cherished memories of my own preacher identity. But the most important thing that Hughie Denton ever did for me was to teach me about financial accountability. He was preaching a revival for me, back in 1972, and I was graduating from college. I was married, had a daughter who was a toddler, and was scraping by financially. Hughie took me to a local store and he purchased a little black ledger and we returned to our house, and sitting at the dining table he began to teach me some of the most basic, and important, principles of personal finance. That changed the course of my life. I am forever indebted to Pastor Hughie Denton for his personal interest in a young preacher, and for the investment of himself that he made into my life. He and Geraldine modeled what pastoring is — shepherding a flock. Gosh, I wish I could hear Geraldine laugh right now. There have been books, tapes, teachers, trainers, professional

FOREWORD

education, seminars, journals, periodicals, professional organizations — all too numerous to even remember, which have impacted my approach to financial planning. To all of them I say, "Thank you."

I am also grateful for the business associates I have learned from and leaned on for more than three decades. Those include William (Buster) Stuart, CFP – my business partner for more than thirty years; Buster and I began working together in 1986. Also, Jimmy Scotchie, CFP – whom I partnered with in preparation for my retirement from the business I began in 1986. Thanks also goes to attorney Mike Jennings – whom I count a friend and know to be an outstanding estate planner. I am grateful to my granddaughter Maggie who spent many tireless hours typing the manuscripts, all while completing her senior year at the University of Alabama and graduating magna cum laude.

To all who desire to be financially free, who are willing to plan, willing to sacrifice, willing to seek and obey God, we prayerfully offer this book. May your journey be an adventure of faith and may you reach a new level of trust in God's ability to make you free.

I offer this thought regarding the question, "Who can benefit from this book?" The most basic answer is that every Christian and non-Christian can benefit from the financial and Biblical wisdom offered in this book. The basic beliefs behind the concepts offered here, including the scriptural references, are universal. I think the concepts can be effective for everyone, regardless of their beliefs, or the presence or absence of any religious beliefs.

Alan Johnston, DMin, CFP®, ChFC, AEP
    Chattanooga, Tennessee

CHAPTER 1

The Promise: Peace and Prosperity

This may seem an unusual beginning for a book on financial planning, but I assure you it is not. While there is no shortage of misinformation and misinterpretation of the meaning of the Bible relative to peace and prosperity, the fact that both those terms are prevalent in scripture cannot be debated. The apostle Paul has much to say on both topics, and perhaps none more telling than found in 1 Timothy 6: 6-11, *"But godliness with contentment is great gain. For we brought nothing into the world, and we can take nothing out of it. But if we have food and clothing, we will be content with that. People who want to get rich fall into temptation and a trap and fall into many foolish and harmful desires that plunge men into ruin and destruction. For the love of money is a root of all kinds of evil. Some people, eager for money have wandered from the faith and pierced themselves with many griefs. But you, man of God, flee from all this, and pursue godliness, faith, love, endurance and gentleness"* (NIV).

The words of Jesus help us reconcile Paul's view and bring balance to our pursuit of peace and prosperity, *"What I'm trying to do here is to get you to relax, to not be so occupied with getting, so you can respond to God's giving. People who don't know God and the way he works fuss over these things, but you know both God and how he works. Steep your life in God-reality, God-initiative, God-provisions. Don't worry about missing out. You'll find all your everyday human concerns will be met"* (Matthew 6: 31-33 MSG).

Relative to this conversation let's make certain that we know that we follow and serve a God of abundance, a God of above and beyond. In Ephesians 3:20 the Bible says, *"Now to Him who is able to do above and beyond all we ask or think according to the power that works in us"* (NIV). There has never been, nor will there ever be, any shortages with God. In matters of finance and management of money (stewardship), the challenge lies within us. The Bible supplies us with ample instruction as to how God operates, and how he wishes us to operate. When we struggle with finances, it most often stems from either our lack of understanding God, or our lack of obedience to God. Verses twenty and twenty-one comprise one of the most magnificent doxologies in the Bible. God has both the aspiration and power to do far, far more than we are even able to comprehend. I cannot think big enough, I cannot ask big enough, to match the desire and ability of God to bless me.

Prosperity

If we are not careful, the word "prosperity" can be a tricky word. Generally, in the Western world, we tend to associate prosperity with how much money and "stuff" a person can accumulate. In that mindset, our personal net worth statement becomes the scorecard for success and prosperity. Using that measuring stick we would quickly label individuals such as Elon Musk, Bill Gates, Jeff Bezos, Warren Buffett – whose names continue to appear on the list of the world's richest people – as unbelievably wealthy and prosperous. The Bible clearly reveals that significant wealth was once in the hands of David, and later his son Solomon. A reading of 1 Chronicles 29, which describes the preparation for building the first Temple, makes it obvious that a massive amount of resources was involved. Using the metric available to us, seeking to understand the values of the gold and silver alone translates into billions of dollars in modern U.S. currency. David and Solomon were billionaires. Upon visiting the vaults of Solomon and viewing his wealth, the Queen of Sheba said, *"The half has not been told."*

It is also important that we have a firm grasp on the Biblical perspective of prosperity. There is the message of the so-called "prosperity gospel" that has often been used to manipulate individual giving. Individuals are urged to use "positive confessions," which implies that one's words have creative power. Such beliefs include the notion that we have the ability, even the right, to make demands of God, especially relative to wealth and health, based on the level of our faith. Many prosperity teachers declare that what you say is what happens to you, therefore, one must stay unwaveringly positive, and that somehow God's blessings hinge on the degree of our faith. Frankly, the Bible (James 4) makes it rather clear that we don't know anything about tomorrow. How could we possibly have the power to create wealth, or anything else with such finite inherent capabilities? Scripture seems to offer a different perspective. Proverbs 23:4-5 gives us some insight into the notion that it is somehow noble to pursue monetary wealth, *"Don't wear yourself out trying to get rich; restrain yourself! Riches disappear in the blink of any eye; wealth sprouts wings and flies off into the wild blue yonder"* (MSG). In their devotional book "Keeping God in the Small Stuff," authors Bruce Bickel and Stan Jantz say, *"The more you have, the more you have to lose. So, you purchase more insurance. But the more insurance you have, the higher the premiums. To afford the higher premiums, you try to make a little more income. With more income, your taxes are higher. To cover the taxes, you buy some rental property. Now you need more insurance. And so, it goes. There is a vicious cycle involved with money...."* No doubt, the amount of wealth we obtain is used by we humans to, at least partially, define success. However, God's opinion of us is not based on typical human value systems. As we will discover, in matters related to money, God is much more concerned about how we handle money (stewardship) versus how much money we have. The story in the Bible wherein Jesus commended the widow and her offering of a few pennies, versus the miserly offerings of the affluent, serves to corroborate my statement.

Chapter seven in this book contains a much more extensive examination of a few of the many scriptures that teach us something about our pursuit and use of money. It remains remarkable to me that Jesus had more to say about the subject of money than he did about heaven or hell. He must have had a good reason for that! As we, throughout this book, seek to use the Bible as our guide, we must be willing to accept what Scripture teaches us. There are both precepts and principles on most subjects in the Bible, including money. Both have great value, and both rightly expect something of us. Precepts involve directives. Read Exodus 20:7-17 and you find the ten major statements: ten commandments. Within those verses are both precepts and principles. For example, verse 13, "you shall not murder," is a precept – a direct command. Easy to understand, right? Can principles be drawn from that simple commandment? Certainly. Principles are not commandments, rather reveal to us how God has arranged the universe around us to operate. Unlike precepts, which come with a penal code, principles – when followed – come with blessings. If I choose to violate or ignore those principles, then I have no right to expect a blessing. We are foolish to think otherwise. Make no mistake, God has a plan to prosper us (Jeremiah 29:11), but we must ensure that we are not confused by our often-earthbound thinking, for we must also remember that God declares, *"For your thoughts are not my thoughts, neither are your ways my ways"* (Isaiah 55:8, NIV). Many simply associate the term "prosperity" with our money, our economic resources. While it includes economic resources, the definition of prosperity does not end there with God. God also wants our soul to prosper, and he certainly wants our mind to prosper. True prosperity envelopes are entire being, our entire existence. If all our thoughts of prospering hinge on our material well-being, it stands to reason that the being that God created – the total person – is lacking, and where lack is found, there is likely the absence of both peace and prosperity.

While our expectations and understanding of prosperity can become skewed, the fact that the Bible teaches us that God wants us to prosper is unmistakable. The Apostle John said, *"...I pray for good fortune in everything you do, and for your good health-that your everyday affairs prosper, as well as your soul!"* (MSG). Proverbs 11:25 says, *"A generous person will prosper..."* (NIV). Proverbs 10:22 (NIV) adds this, *"The blessing of the Lord brings wealth...."* Solomon provides this, no doubt from personal experience, *"Moreover, when God gives someone wealth and possessions and the ability to enjoy them, to accept their lot and be happy in their toil – this is a gift of God."* (Ecclesiastes 5:19, NIV)

Later, in chapter seven, we will more fully explore these concepts as we seek a greater grasp on Biblical truth. Yes, God wants us to prosper, but let's not limit our thinking about prosperity to the financial world. To do so would be to greatly limit our knowledge of God, and thereby fail to appreciate the vastness of His blessings. There are verses that cause us to know that God wants us to prosper, but at the same time we must affirm that prosperity can include finances but is much more. In 2 Corinthians 8:9 the Bible says, *"For you know the grace of our Lord Jesus Christ, that though he was rich, he for your sake became poor, so that you by his poverty might become rich (NIV).* I believe that can encompass everything; after all, God wants us to prosper physically, mentally, emotionally, spiritually – and, yes, He will provide for our financial well-being as well.

In the growing political divide in America, we might think that the long held notion of the American dream has vanished, or at the very least become tarnished. That dream includes the ideal of an equal opportunity for peace and prosperity, not to be confused with equal outcomes. Because of our individuality it is foolish to believe that we can legislate equal outcomes. Human nature does not support equal outcomes. No amount of legislation can turn us into robots who are programed for equal outcomes. Our American ideals do support the belief that all Americans are entitled to an equal opportunity to find genuine peace and prosperity. Why interject this thought into a conversation regarding prosperity? I believe the so-called prosperity gospel has generated such widespread appeal because it plays into the American dream – riches for all. My fear is that this perversion of the gospel brings with it an emphasis on materialism by encouraging us to invest much of our time in the pursuit of riches. The culture around us is firmly addicted to material wealth, and we have preachers who peddle the intoxicating cocktail of materialism and consumerism. Christians are encouraged to put their hope in money with distorted messages to name it and claim it, sadly, further attaching us to a doomed world, clearly contradicting the statement of scripture, "you are not of this world."

John Piper said, "God deals in the currency of grace, not money...." Money is the currency of human resources. So, the heart that loves money is a heart that pins its hopes, and purses its pleasures, and puts its trust in what human resources can offer. So, the love of money is virtually the same as faith in money – belief (trust, confidence, assurance) that money will meet your needs and make you happy." Clearly the American culture is saturated with this belief system, but we should not allow it to invade the spiritual turf of our churches. Jesus taught that our giving should be done without hoping for anything in return (Luke 10:35). On the other hand, the gospel of prosperity places great emphasis on giving that is motivated by the promise of a multiplied return. Jesus certainly seemed to have a great deal to say about motives, as did the Apostle Paul. We must be careful that we are not making the pursuit of material things and physical wellbeing ends in themselves. Bible teacher and writer Warren Wiersbe says of this wealth gospel (he refers to it as the success gospel) that it is "perfectly suited to our American society that worships health, wealth and happiness." Gordon Fee, theologian, college professor, and minister in the Assemblies of God church made this observation, "American Christianity is rapidly being infected by...the so-called wealth and health gospel – although it has very little of the character of the gospel in it. In its more brazen forms...it simply says, 'Serve God and get rich'...in its more respectable form...it builds fifteen-million-dollar Cathedrals to the glory of affluent suburban Christianity." We don't need preaching and teaching that leads us to believe that God is a heavenly ATM machine. This distortion of the true gospel places its rewards theology on the here and now, whereas Jesus spoke often of rewards in the future tense. Missing from the prosperity gospel is a biblical explanation of pain and suffering. For reasons best known to God alone, He often chooses not to protect believers from the customary problems of life. Across the generations God's people are plagued and hurt by discrimination, disease, poverty, injustices and out right persecution. Dare we tell the afflicted that their lack of faith is their problem. Job's friends presented that belief to Job. Yet, we know the testimony of scripture that Job was an entirely righteous person. God warns us about allowing money to take up too much space in our life. Sadly, some preachers make it all about the money. Jesus repeatedly cautioned that we must keep our guard up against the tentacles of greed.

John Wesley understood the human tendency to yield to the temptation that we often flirt with as resources begin to flow into our lives. Because of his gift as a writer, he was blessed with an income that far exceeded his needs. His approach to his prosperity appears to be far different that many of us, for he said, "Money never stays with me. It would burn me if it did. I throw it out of my hands as soon as possible, lest it find its way into my heart." His goal became to give to the extent that he would die empty handed, and he did just that. Wesley understood that what counts, what lasts, what is eternal, what has a value that will never diminish, is not any prosperity that we can accumulate in the here and now.... rather, it is only that we have sent ahead into the real Kingdom that has the qualities of being recession proof and inexhaustible. Only those deposits of our treasure are eternally quantifiable in the realm of the heavens.

Furthermore, in our seeking clarification on matters of prosperity we must remind ourselves that one of the divine attributes of God is His goodness. We say it all the time in church – "God is good, all the time." Indeed! However, we should understand that God's mercy extends to those who trust and obey God, but God's goodness is not limited to only those who trust and obey. God deals bountifully with the just and unjust. Jesus said, "...*for He is kind to the ungrateful and the evil.*" (Luke 6:35) In Matthew 5:45 Jesus said, "*For He makes his sun rise on the evil and on the good and sends rain on the just and the unjust.*" God has never been or will ever be more good because we are good, just as He is not less good to those who are evil. It was Augustine who said, "Good for evil: that is divine." You and I are not prone to operate that way, but such is the very nature of God. Such goodness is one of His divine attributes, and no one is excluded from that goodness.

In gaining a fuller understanding of how wonderfully God provides for us, carefully read chapter five in this book. To increase awareness relative to what God's stewardship expectations of us are, carefully read chapter thirteen of this book. Never forget that the full realization of prosperity and understanding its implications is first and foremost triggered not by giving, but by obedience. As I discuss in another chapter it was Abraham who first identified God as Jehovah-Jireh...the God who provides. In the God-Abraham encounter in Genesis 22 there is certainly sacrificial giving involved. But the willingness of Abraham to make an offering was preceded by his obedience. What God ultimately provided - the highly symbolic substitutionary death of a ram - was the result of Abraham's unflinching faith in God. Abraham had to abandon everything to the will of God. Abraham provides us with the complete example of surrender. The place where Jehovah-Jireh is found in the New Testament is in Philippians 4:19, *"But my God will supply all your needs...."* I have taught the book of Philippians many times, and it is the one letter that Paul wrote that is filled with joy and very, very little that even remotely resembles a rebuke. Why? Because that church, those Christians, had fully surrendered their lives in obedience to Christ. Paul told them that their lives of surrender and sacrifice had become a sweet smell to God, and that He was well pleased with their sacrifice. Wow! The texture of their lives, their character, their commitment opened the windows of heaven to bless them.

So then, what can we conclude on this subject of prosperity. We can rightly conclude that God has plans for us, and that those plans include *"plans for peace and well-being, not disaster, to give you a future and a hope."* (Jer. 29:11 AMP) I can't speak for you, but for me that sounds like God's plan of prosperity.

Peace

If we lose sight of our identity in Christ it becomes an almost certainty that we will lose our emotional and spiritual peace of mind. An oft quoted, and well-beloved verse from the New Testament can serve as the foundation of our ability to, in Christ, remain peaceful when chaos surrounds us: *"And my God will supply every need of yours according to his riches in glory in Christ Jesus."* (Philippians 4:19) Don't miss the direction of this promise. It clearly defines a giver and a recipient. You and I are on the receiving end of the promise, and it is God alone who is the giver. Abraham encountered this same God and declared him to be Jehovah-Jireh, which means "the Lord will provide." That compound name, used by Abraham, for God can also mean "the Lord will see to it." Oh my! How marvelous. Our God, who is our provider, is more than capable of "seeing" to our every need. That means that when Isaac, Abraham's son, asked about the need for a sacrifice, his dad simply replied, "the Lord will see to it." Does it not still work that way? When God sees my need, he sees to it that I have what I need. I can have no shortage that God cannot supply. We can have no problem that leads to panic in heaven. Peace prevails in our hearts as we surrender to his sovereignty. This promise comes to us without limits as to its depth. How many needs can God supply? ALL. God has "all his riches in glory" at his fingertips and therefore is more than ready to interject himself in our lives. As I write these pages, America finds itself in chaotic times. An ever, overreaching government, rapidly rising inflation, shortages of staple goods, rising crime rates, an escalating drug epidemic define these times, volatility for the stock market, housing prices rising faster than the financial ability to own a house. Yet may we not forget God is the creator and administrator of this world. He owns it all, and according to Paul in Colossians he is keeping it together. Not only does he own it all, but he also directs the distribution of all resources. No wonder Paul said that he had learned how to be content. It is here that we must decide. Do we believe God? Do we trust God? Is he able to meet all my needs? If we answer with a heart of faith and say yes, then we are assured of "*...the peace of God which surpasses all understanding, will guard your hearts and minds in Christ Jesus.*"

The writer of Hebrews said, "*Now without faith it is impossible to please God....*" (Hebrews 11:6) I often hear Christians say "I love God, but I have trouble trusting Him." What? Frankly, if that is true you are not in fellowship with God – because your lack of faith displeases God. My walk of faith has never eliminated any problems. However, it is my faith that has enabled me to keep trusting God when surrounded by those problems.

In John's gospel Jesus had much to say about peace as defined by God. In John 14:27 Jesus said, "*My peace I leave with you; my peace I give to you. Not as the world gives do I give to you.*" What is this peace that Jesus has promised. To fully grasp the gracious splendor of that peace we need to fully appreciate two aspects of peace as taught in the New Testament. There is both the "Peace of God," and certainly "Peace with God." In Romans 5:1 the Apostle Paul introduces us to the meaning of experiencing peace with God. Scripture says, "*Therefore, since we have been justified by faith, we have peace with God through our Lord Jesus Christ."* This is an obvious reference to salvation by grace. Through no efforts of our own, and certainly not based on any merits earned, we *"... by grace you have been saved through faith. And this is not your own doing; it is the gift of God...."* Based on that transforming experience we have peace, because as Paul said, *"There is therefore no condemnation for those who are in Christ Jesus."* Clearly, we are peace with God upon the confession of our sins and believe that Jesus Christ died for our sins, and we trust Him to save us from our sinful self. Having made peace with God, we put ourselves in position to experience the peace of God. Paul described the peace of God as not *"being anxious about anything... the peace of God, which surpasses all understanding, will guard your hearts and minds in Christ Jesus."* The Message Bible, using those same verses, provides remarkable clarity about the joy we experience when we are resting in the peace of God, *"Don't fret or worry. Instead of worrying, pray...before you know it, a sense of God's wholeness, everything coming together for good, will come and settle you down. It's wonderful what happens when Christ displaces worry in your life."* (Phil. 4:6-7)

What could be more settling, more encouraging, more comforting, than knowing that God – through the portal of His peace – builds a wall around us and apparently assigns a heavenly guard to watch over us, preventing anything from approaching us that would disturb or worry us. Don't you see, living an anxiety free life is not dependent on what I can or should do. Anxiety free living is the work of the Holy Spirit in my life. The prophet Isaiah had that in mind when he said, *"You keep him in perfect peace whose mind is stayed on you, because he trusts in you."* (Isa. 26:3) We would do well to heed the simple, yet profound, words of Jesus, *"Let not your heart be troubled...."*

CHAPTER 2

The Pathway: What is Financial Planning?

While none of us has any guarantee of tomorrow, nor do we claim to know what the future holds, we do have dreams and plans. We talk of buying a new home, sending our children to college, starting a business, taking a cruise, and enjoying a comfortable retirement. Most people can verbally express what they would like to see happen during their lifetime, yet only three percent of Americans reach retirement financially independent. The reason? The lack of planning, which includes setting goals and establishing priorities. Without precisely defined objectives and a written game plan which leads progressively toward those objectives, there is little hope for financial security and financial independence.

In my more than half a century of work as a minister, licensed counselor and Certified Financial Planner, I know of no greater need than for individuals and families to get their financial house in order. The lack of financial planning can lead to stress in the family, a sense of guilt and failure, a feeling of being out of control, and it can dishonor God. Financial planning at some level is an absolute must.

ALAN JOHNSTON

GETTING IT TOGETHER

Upon meeting a person for the first time, following the formal introductions, the first question usually asked is, "What do you do?" When I'm asked that question and I tell people that I am a financial planner, many will then ask what exactly that means. I've tried to explain in a variety of ways, some complicated and some very simple, what financial planning involves. Perhaps one of my clients said it best. The couple had agreed that they needed a sense of direction in their financial lives, and I was seeking to explain what the financial planning process would do for them. Then, like a light had gone on, the wife looked up at me and with a real sense of enthusiasm said, "Oh, you're going to help us get our stuff together!" I thought, yeah, that's it, financial planning is just getting our financial "stuff" together.

One textbook defines financial planning as the development and implementation of total, coordinated plans for the achievement of one's overall financial objectives. The two key words are overall and coordinated. In other words, "getting it all together." Many individuals engage in piecemeal financial planning which tends to solve only some of the problems. Comprehensive financial planning focuses on an individual's objectives as the starting point in financial planning, and then moves toward solutions using a variety of instruments to systematically address all the needs of the individual.

While every situation is different, and a variety of instruments will likely be used to help an individual achieve their objectives, comprehensive financial planning will generally be identified as encompassing key areas:
    1. Present Financial Situation
       Income - Cash Flow
       Savings - Cash Reserves
       Debt repayment
       Budgeting (Spending plan)
       Net Worth
    2. Protection Planning (Insurance)
       Disability Income (Disability insurance)

Premature Death (Life insurance)
   Medical Coverage (Health insurance)
   Property and Liability (Various forms of insurance)
3. Wealth Accumulation (Saving/investing for a particular purpose)
   Education
   Special Purposes (Start a business, buy a home or car, etc.)
   Investment Strategies (Risk tolerance, Timeline, Portfolio)
4. Tax Planning
   Reduction of Tax Burden – Keep more of what you earn
5. Retirement Planning
   Developing a retirement portfolio
   Charitable Distributions
   Retirement Income – Strategies and sustainability of income
   Health Care and Long-Term Care
6. Estate Planning (Legacy Planning)
   Wills and Trusts
   Charitable Gifts
   Endowments and Donor Advised Funds

Often financial planners, working with attorneys, accountants, bankers and other professional advisors can provide a team approach in addressing a person's financial goals. This systematic, logical approach eliminates the gaps created by a piecemeal approach.

BUILDING BLOCKS

Our homes did not suddenly spring up one day. At some point there was a great deal of planning that was done before the first brick was put in place. An architect likely spent hours designing a plan for that house. Financial freedom becomes a reality when one takes the time to design and implement a financial plan.

Two important points need to be noted. First, I am convinced that one's financial plan needs to be written. Much more will be said about this in a later chapter. However, until those goals and objectives are on "paper," we will likely make little commitment toward reaching those goals.

Secondly, it should be noted that a sound financial plan needs to have a balanced financial philosophy as its foundation. There is a page in the appendix titled "Four Cornerstones" that illustrates this point. These four cornerstones serve as the very foundation upon which we will build our financial house.

ONLY THE RICH

Who is it that needs to engage in financial planning? Perhaps many think that financial planning is only for the rich, or for those whose income has reached six figure incomes. The truth is that most people need financial planning to some degree. Often those of modest means lack information about financial planning and therefore miss the opportunity to apply sound and proven techniques that could enable one to achieve financial independence. It has been suggested that less affluent people need planning more than those with greater wealth because each dollar means relatively more to them.

Certainly, it should be recognized that neglecting to plan carries a very high price tag. The failure to plan could leave your family inadequately protected from catastrophic events and risks. It could mean having to make unwanted compromises because there was not enough money set aside for education or retirement. It could also mean paying too much in taxes or having your estate settled against what would have been your wishes. Whatever financial planning might cost; it will be far more costly not to plan. Just before the beginning of my Senior year in high school I celebrated my seventeenth birthday. There was a war being fought in Vietnam which meant the military was sending more and more young men to war. My thought process was to join the Army while completing my Senior year, and my parents agreed to the idea, all based on the notion that it might give me a bit more control over my future. During the induction process I reported to the facility in Montgomery, AL through which all incoming recruits were given a physical examination to determine fitness for military service. Since football and track had long been a part of life, I imagined that passing such an exam would be a snap. Imagine my dismay when told I had been disqualified for military service. The reason I was not allowed to join the Army was the presence of a heart murmur – a murmur that no doctor had ever detected before. Following that experience my mother made certain that I had regular meetings with doctors, and for me the habit of having at least an annual physical examination became routine. Later in life I did in fact have a heart attack and bypass surgery for five blocked arteries. I am convinced that my regular visits to the doctor, along with all the tests and procedures, is one of the reasons I am still alive today. What might have happened if I had simply ignored certain symptoms? What if I had brushed aside the idea that I needed a physical exam, after all, most of the time I felt okay. Now let's take what I said about my physical health and apply it to my financial health. Individuals who brush aside symptoms, who ignore the advice of their doctor, who indulge too often, who show little discipline in exercising and eating habits, are flirting with a disaster. At best incapacitation, at worst death. Physical neglect brings its own punitive outcomes, and the same can be said of our financial well-being. A laissez-faire attitude toward our financial lives is an open invitation to disappointment and despair.

Planning is a must. Jesus pointed to this fact in Luke 14:28-30 when he talked about an individual who began construction on a building only to run out of money before completing the project. Jesus said we must plan so that we can see our objectives become reality. Business schools, motivational speakers, psychologist, statisticians, financial planners…and on, and on goes the list…of those who propose that goal setting, accompanied by a written plan for reaching that goal, exponentially improves the probability of reaching that goal. The old adage, "aim for nothing and you are assured of hitting nothing," rings true. I read a study on goal setting and goal-achievement done by the Statistical Brain Research Institute which proved rather revealing:

- 45% of Americans usually make goals.
- 17% of Americans infrequently make goals.
- 38% of Americans never make goals.

Those stats mean that about 62% of Americans make a stab at goal setting, while 38% never set goals. Another measure in that study tracked how far individuals got in "working" toward their goals before giving up on the goal. Of those who do set goals, 25% never make it through the first week. Only 62% of the goal-setters make it past thirty days and only 46% of them make it past the six-month mark. The research indicates that only 8% of those who set goals, reach their goals. Many years ago, while working alongside the American Express Financial Advisors company, I learned the value of setting SMART goals. A SMART goal will be specific. In planning your financial life each goal must be specific as to the what, when, how and how much criteria. What is your objective (car, house, start a business, pay for college, etc.)? When will you need the money? How much money will you need (don't ignore inflation)? How will you save and invest to best ensure that you have the desired outcome at the right time? Your goal will also need to be measurable. Some visible, readily attainable means of tracking progress will be necessary. If you fall behind, get off track, what will you do to get your plan back on track? Every goal must be actionable. Part of the planning process includes identifying what actions must be taken in order to accomplish a stated goal. Just before Christmas 2022 I decided that my physical health needed some attention relative to some extra baggage that came along during the prolonged COVID shutdowns. I decided that I wanted to lose at least twenty-five pounds (which could get me around my high school weight). In order to do that I would need a plan. I could not continue to eat what I was eating, nor continue a somewhat sedentary lifestyle. I could think about it. I could talk about it. I could even visualize it. But until I developed a set of actions regarding food intake and exercise nothing would change. I can tell you that I set a goal, developed a plan, and seven weeks into the plan I have lost fifteen pounds. I finally stopped talking about what I needed to do and acted. Any plan also needs to be realistic. Sure, we want to challenge ourselves with our goals, but at the same time we must be wise. I have had individuals share goals that are unreachable based on their current circumstances. Such goals will quickly lead to discouragement and eventually quitting altogether. SMART goals are also timebound. In financial planning many goals are long-range, but even those goals are timebound. Some goals are more immediate. Good planning always includes setting dates. For my weight loss goal, I set six months as my target date. I track my outcome daily (measure). I adjust as needed. Our life goals, no matter the component of life, can be, and likely should be submitted to the SMART goal test.

PRODUCT OR PROCESS

Any product is typically an end unto itself. Since financial planning is continuous and never truly complete it would seem better to consider it a process rather than a product. Financial planning is in fact a series of steps that move in cyclical fashion. The process involves the translation of personal goals into specific plans and ultimately into some type of financial arrangement to implement those plans. Financial planning is that process that enables us to identify our personal goals, develop strategies that will direct us toward the achievement of those goals, and periodically monitor our process toward our desired end results.

The first step in the process involves assessing your present situation and collecting certain financial data into an understandable and manageable format. This information will lay the groundwork for the comprehensive plan that is to be developed. In some ways it is like the conversation I have at least annually with my doctor. He begins with a series of questions, accompanied by a lot of notetakings on his part.

The second step involves clarifying your personal financial objectives and establishing some initial goals. The failure to set goals – as we have already stated - is clearly one of the reasons many fail financially. Goals need to be concise and specific. For example, it's not enough to say, "I want to retire comfortably." That statement is too vague, too nebulous. Instead, one could state, "I want to retire at age 62 and have a monthly income of $5,000.00." This step continues until all a person's goals have been clarified and recorded.

Comprehensive analysis of a person's present situation in relation to the goals of that individual is the third step of the process. Once again, using the analogy of my visits to the doctor, he will – depending on what issues present themselves - order various tests. Often lab work is needed, ex-rays are ordered. Certain presenting medical factors could call for more sophisticated analysis. Financial planning processes often follow a similar path. Typically, areas will be identified that are areas of strength while other areas of one's financial situation will be identified as areas for improvement. It is here that alternatives are considered for reaching one's goals.

Step number four brings about the development of the plan along with the alternatives that may exist. This is akin to the prescription and treatment phase used by my physician. In financial planning recommendations are made that relate to the specific objectives of the individual, family or business. Implementation of the recommendations begin at this point and of course progresses over time.

The final step in the process is in fact not the final step. This step calls for monitoring and reviewing the financial plan. As circumstances and life events change, the plan must flex with the changes. Events such as marriages, births, divorces, death, career changes and of course economic conditions all impact one's financial life and must be considered. The ongoing review process is a vital link in successful financial planning.

WHY PLAN?

Ultimately the use of our resources becomes a matter of stewardship, which will be discussed in a later chapter. We must understand that no matter how wealthy a person might become, there are still limits to that person's resources. Only God has an unlimited supply. Therefore, since we are all operating with limited resources, developing a financial plan to best use those resources becomes a matter of stewardship. A plan will put order into our financial lives, free us from a great deal of frustration and confusion, enable us to be more productive and ultimately, honor God.

At some point most individuals will want to seek the counsel of a knowledgeable and trusted advisor. The Bible says in Proverbs 15:22 (NIV): *"Plans fail for lack of counsel, but with many advisors they succeed."*

I strongly urge everyone to consider using a professional financial advisor to assist in the development and implementation of their financial plan. Certified Financial Planners (CFP) and Chartered Financial Consultants (ChFC) are some of the most highly trained and skilled financial professionals in the marketplace. They are held to a rigorous Code of Ethics, subject to the highest compliance standards, and they are held to the regulatory mandates of a "fiduciary," which means they must always put the interests of their clients above all other interests. For Christians it can make sense to seek out a financial planner who has a Biblical worldview. For many years I have belonged to an organization of Christians financial professions known as "Kingdom Advisors." I joined many years ago when it was still known as Christian Financial Professionals Network. Members are trained to, and pledge to, provide financial planning advice based on a Biblical worldview. It has enabled many of us to correctly make the connection between the Bible and the discipline of finance. Certification requires educational training, annual continuing education, and compliance to Christian ideals and values. Naturally, there many fine Christians who have chosen not to affiliate with Kingdom Advisors. The key is finding a good match between advisor and client, and for we Christians, our faith and values are a vital component of who we are – thus, the importance of having the right relationships. For example, we have the current drift of many "woke" and liberal leaning financial firms – along with our Federal Government – who want the so-called ESG standards applied to all businesses in America, including how you and I invest for retirement and our futures. ESG is the acronym for environment, social and governance and it is being pushed on companies and they the choose to do business. The not yet spoken, but highly implied, message is that current business practices in America are corrupt in ways that result in grave social injustice - and those businesses need to be penalized if they don't fall in line with the ESG standards. I include this "rant" because if it continues unabated it could impact every retirement savings plan in America. So...when it comes to financial decision making, doesn't it make sense to find someone whose values resemble my own? Perhaps we would do well to consider the Apostle Paul's caution about marriage, *"Do not be yoked together with unbelievers. For what do righteousness and wickedness have in common?"* (NIV) Many years ago, as I was in the early stages of "building" my business, we had hired a young man who had graduated from West Point and had recently completed his military career. One afternoon as I sat in our office – with my door open – I could hear that young man talking on the telephone with a client. He was berating the client and telling them that they were giving too much money to their church and that the money should be directed to their own financial needs. As soon as he hung the phone up, we had a lengthy conversation about values based financial planning and investing. Every person who is licensed to offer investment securities to a client operates under a far-reaching mandate known as, "Know your client." It means just that.... don't recommend anything until you (the planner) know every financial detail of a client's life. For this conversation I think we can turn that mandate around.... "Know your financial planner." Do they truly value what you value, believe what you believe? Yes, it matters.

CHAPTER 3

The Problem: Roadblocks to Financial Freedom

A most frustrating experience took place one Sunday as we left church following the worship service. We had an engagement in another location within the city, and I had mentally traced my route along familiar streets and in my mind had clocked the driving time. Everything would be just fine I told myself, we would arrive with minutes to spare. Church was dismissed a bit later than usual, but I reminded myself that given the route I had chosen we would still be on time. This was confirmed as even the traffic lights seemed to cooperate by giving us a green light at each intersection. Then it happened! I made a right-hand turn onto the side street on which my destination was located. Within about four blocks there it was! There sat a huge earth moving machine guarding an open ditch across the street and a big orange sign that declared "Detour." Okay, we'll still make it I reassured myself, but there was a new problem. The sign said detour, however, there were no markings or arrows to direct me as to which way to travel. Now not having enough time to turn back and go another route I decided to drive off onto an unfamiliar side street thinking that my instincts would guide me through these never traveled streets. To my dismay, after driving several blocks I discovered the street to be a dead end. After several right turns and then left turns and more dead ends I finally found my way back to the street from which I had detoured.

However, I was now frustrated, agitated and twenty minutes late. How helpful it would have been, I thought, if only someone had provided some directional signs to assist motorist around that roadblock. A great deal of anxiety could have been avoided (there was no GPS).

This true story relates perfectly to our financial lives. I have never met any person who planned to fail financially. I've never had a client say to me, "I want you to help me lose money." There has yet to be anyone say, "Alan, my goal is to be broke when I reach age sixty-five." Yet many do fail financially. Research indicates that only 3% of Americans reach financial independence by age sixty-five. What happens to the other 97% of the population? They don't intend to fail or in some way fall short of their objectives, yet they do. The reason is that they fail to consider the roadblocks that they are certain to encounter, and they fail to have a financial road map that can direct them around the roadblocks. Financial planning provides a flexible map that can enable one to steer safely around the barriers that prevent so many from achieving financial freedom.

WHY PEOPLE FAIL

<u>LACK OF GOALS:</u> Far too few individuals take the time to think through their financial objectives. We need to have clear, precise, and measurable financial goals. Furthermore, these goals need to be written. Our commitment to the goal is likely to be greater if we've taken the time to put them on paper. Our goals become our guide for saving and investing.

<u>INADEQUATE INSURANCE:</u> You must understand certain basic insurance principles, for insurance provides an important means of meeting the financial objectives of most people. There are various forms of risk and their magnitude and how we manage those risks can literally mean the difference in financial ruin in a catastrophic sense and financial security. Risk exposure must be analyzed and then evaluated to determine the amount of control one might have over the risk. Risk will either be avoided, reduced, retained, or transferred. This can become a rather perplexing task and too many people just avoid or neglect the issue and are unknowingly courting disaster.

PIECEMEAL APPROACH: Life can seem to be a series of financial events. In fact, it often is just that. Early in my young adult life I made a financial decision to purchase an automobile. In so doing our local banker (a longtime family friend) made a loan to me to cover the purchase of the car. There it was my first official financial relationship. I had a banker! Shortly thereafter I made the decision to purchase a small life insurance policy for which I paid monthly premiums. That meant I had a new financial relationship with the insurance company. This scene repeated itself many times as my situation grew and changed and I became acquainted with and in need of the services of real estate agents, an attorney, an accountant, and even a securities broker. I had solid financial relationships with all of these people. Then one day it suddenly dawned on me that I had all of these people and events impacting my financial life, but no one was coordinating what was taking place. Each seemed to be acting independently of the other without any real knowledge of what the other advisors were recommending. That is what is meant by a piecemeal approach. Financial planning is the means by which all of these factors and events related to one's financial life are coordinated into a comprehensive approach. The piecemeal approach lacks a real strategy, whereas comprehensive personal financial planning develops a total and coordinated strategy for reaching one's objectives.

LACK OF KNOWLEDGE: Stocks, bonds, mutual funds, annuities, limited partnerships, futures, real estate, real rate of return, tax equivalent yield, internal rate of return, yield to maturity, blue chip, emerging growth, margins, options, tax shelters, precious metals, cryptocurrency, international investments. Whew! The list just goes on and on. How can a person possibly know what is right in each situation when it comes to making money management decisions? Certainly, every situation is unique in some way and there are many options available and so many variables impacting our decisions it would seem prudent for the individual to seek the counsel of a knowledgeable and trusted advisor who has the ability and patience to develop a financial plan which can enable the individual to then make informed and knowledgeable decisions. The Financial Planning Association is the leading organization for CFP's (Certified Financial Planners), The National Association of Personal Financial Advisors, along with the

National Association for Insurance and Financial Advisors are organizations which promote the education of the public in money matters and who work to ensure the quality practice of financial planning by those who engage in planning for the public. In addition to these, and specifically related to the Christian faith, is the organization I mentioned in a previous chapter, Kingdom Advisors. These organizations are available to assist anyone locate a knowledgeable advisor.

<u>FAILURE TO APPLY TAX LAWS PROPERLY:</u> Congress continues to change the rules and it seems that with every new promise to make tax laws more simple and fairer, they become increasingly complex, and the tax burden becomes greater. This topic will be explored more fully in a later chapter, but the point here is simply that many people pay more than they must in federal income taxes either because they don't understand the laws, or they wrongly apply the laws. A financial planner along with one's tax advisor can devise the best plan for avoiding any unnecessary taxes.

<u>PROCRASTINATION:</u> Perhaps now we have come to the single most significant reason why people fail financially. How many times have you looked back and said, "I wish," "I shoulda," I coulda?" We are told that hindsight is twenty-twenty. Most of us would change several things if we could. Well, we can't. However, we don't have to sit idly by and watch the future pass us by. Especially our financial future. The single biggest step in financial planning is getting started. Don't fall into that trap of "When.........then I'll do financial planning." That time will never come. It will always be after Christmas, or after-tax time, or after school starts, or after little league is over, or after vacation, or after I get a raise, or after I get out of debt. You will always be able to find an excuse to postpone doing what needs to be done. Do you want to enjoy financial freedom? Then you must begin the process and stop procrastinating.

COMMON PROBLEMS

Further exploration of the roadblocks to financial freedom leads us to the realization that there are certain problems common to all that should be addressed. Failure to address these issues could lead to serious financial difficulties.

NOT ENOUGH MONEY: Perhaps the most obvious of all is just having too little money left at the end of the check. It just seems there is never enough to go around. Then, after all, how much is enough?

TOO MUCH MONEY: Rarely does one find that person who says I have too much money. Yet if you have a few dollars, several thousand dollars or, hundreds of thousands of dollars is not the point. It is what we do with what we have. Even if we have very limited resources and have not planned in such a way to maximize those dollars, then we have too much money that is not working to our advantage.

INFLATION: For many years inflation, while always present, remained relatively low. We had the double-digit inflation of the early eighties. The somewhat tame inflation numbers of more recent years did not seem so bad, especially if compared to the fourteen percent of a decade past. Consider, however that at five percent, it only takes about fourteen years for the cost of all the goods, services, and products that we use to double in cost. Low inflation or high inflation.... What is certain that the cost to live has and will continue to rise. At the time I am writing this book we have once again entered a period of high inflation, which is impacting almost everything that touches our daily lives. Inflation occurs when the price of money begins to fall. Money is a commodity and is priced as such based-on supply and demand. Economist Milton Friedman said, "Inflation is always and everywhere a monetary phenomenon in the sense that it is and can only be produced by a more rapid increase in the quantity of money than in output." Government has only three ways to fund their spending. The first two, taxes and borrowing are commonly used by our own government. The third method a government could use to meet their obligations is to print money. During the 2020 pandemic, that shut the country down, the deficit spending of the U.S. soared, and the national debt grew by more than $9 trillion between 2017 and 2022. The government began handing out relief money like a clown throwing candy from a parade float. People stopped working, and many have not yet gone back. The inflationary result was not seen immediately, but it had to happen, and it did. By December 2021 consumer prices had seen the largest increase in more than forty years. The flood of cash that made its way into the mailboxes and checking accounts of Americans is the prime culprit for the inflation still being experienced in 2023. Combine that with the loss of production in gas and oil and disruptions in supply chains, and we are as Friedman said, creating too much money, and predictably the outcome is inflation.

<u>DEFLATION:</u> As we experienced for many years, we found ourselves in a double bind. For a decade, even though mild, inflation continued to erode our purchasing power while at the same time the interest rates that we could earn on our money reached historical lows. Though prices did not decrease, interest rates have recently been at all-time lows creating a new set of problems for many who are somewhat dependent on interest earnings for income.

<u>DYING TOO SOON:</u> The ultimate realization of our financial goals depends on our living and working long enough to save and invest sufficient resources to enable us to accomplish our goals. My family and I have numerous goals that we hope to see achieved in the years to come. For years those goals were predicated on the fact that I would live and continue to earn an income. Without proper planning, many of our family's goals will go to the grave with us.

<u>LIVING TOO LONG:</u> The greatest concern of the retired clients that I have worked with as their financial planner has been the concern that they might outlive their income. As we live longer, and as costs continue to climb, especially health care, this is a legitimate concern.

There are numerous other problems that must be addressed during financial planning; however, these six problems raise some of the key issues with which every person serious about financial freedom must concern themselves. These issues and life events can alter the course of our financial future and we dare not leave it to chance.

Planning is not easy; it requires commitment and discipline, without which financial independence is not found. Of discipline the Bible says, *"No discipline seems pleasant at the time, but painful. Later on, however, it produces a harvest of righteousness and peace for those who have been trained by it." (Hebrews 12:11 NIV)*

Relative to financial health debt is our mortal enemy. Long ago, as a college freshman, I was introduced to what has been called the "magic of compound interest." Pretty basic stuff, right? We save some of our money, and we earn interest (or perhaps dividends) on our money. Then we are suddenly earning interest on the money we saved, plus, we are earning interest on the accumulated interest....and, the cycle continues. Granted, for some time now interest paid on savings has been rather low. Although, at the time I am writing this we are in a phase of rising interest rates and my cash reserve account is earning 3% interest. But my point here is that consumer debt is the magic of compound interest in reverse. Many households are bombarded each month with a stack of credit related bills (or more so these days, a seemingly never-ending electronic list of credit bills). Credit cards, mortgage payments, automobile payments, student loans, bank loans, second mortgages and home equity lines of credit, consumer debts – not to mention all the other routine household expenses. Those credit related expenses likely come at a high cost.... compound interest in reverse. Thus, this revolving door of credit, and the debt that comes with it becomes our adversary in our search for financial independence. It is often the greatest obstacle to financial peace and prosperity. Later in this book there is an entire chapter devoted to this single issue.

Navigating these numerous problems requires planning, perseverance, resolve (discipline) and sacrifice. Is it work? Yes! Is it hard? Yes! Will there be setbacks? Yes? Is it worth the effort? Absolutely!

CHAPTER 4

The Peril: The Danger of Debt

Of all the roadblocks to financial peace and prosperity, this danger of debt can be both tantalizing and insidious at one and the same time. There is a certain street in my city that is cluttered by check-into-cash businesses, pay-day loan companies, title loan establishments and pawn shops. There is also an abundance of rent-to-own stores selling furniture, electronics and appliances. They are surrounded by billboards boasting "Buy Now – Pay Later." "No Money Down – Easy Credit." Let's get real, there is no such thing as easy credit. The Bible offers this simple commentary on the subject, "*The rich rules over the poor, and the borrower is the slave of the lender.*" You just thought slavery ended in America ended in 1865. We are a nation of debtors. As 2022 wound down and the rising cost of almost everything needed for our everyday lives, the pressure to "make ends meet" continues to rise. At the end of 2022, CNBC reported that 63% of Americans were living paycheck to paycheck. Even some with incomes in excess of $100,000.00 reported living paycheck to paycheck. That means that our spending continues to outpace our income. The two most apparent options to that dilemma includes spending from one's cash reserves or using more credit. Credit card use in the last quarter of 2022 rose 15%, the largest annual jump in 20 years. That is coupled with the fact that credit card interest rates rose more than 19% on average (all time high) and are still rising. As we might imagine, these facts lead to the next fact – 32% of all consumers report now saving less money. In these times of high inflation, market volatility, combined with soaring real estate and automobile costs – how can we ignore putting our financial plan in some documented format (paper/digital) and get the help of a financial planner who can help steer the financial ship into calmer waters.

DROWNING IN DEBT

Some years ago, while walking across our church parking lot I stopped, starred and laughed. The rear bumper of a car had a sticker on it that read, "I Owe, I Owe, It's Off to Work I Go." Funny, yes, but at the same time it is a sobering and sad commentary on the state of our nation and our personal lives. At the end of the third quarter in 2022 the credit card balances of American's totaled $925 billion. That represents a $38 billion increase since the end of the first quarter. At the end of that same third quarter the total household debt here in the U.S. reached $16.51 trillion. Nerdwallet reports (January 10, 2023) that the average American household owes $165,388.00 in debt. Of that, the average revolving credit balance was $7,486.00 and the total household credit card balance was $17,066.00. Add an average mortgage balance of $222,592.00, an average auto loan balance of $28,975.00 and top it off with an average student loan balance of $58,238.00. It is predicted that the U.S. households that carry credit card debt will pay an average of $1,380.00 in interest this year (assuming rates don't go higher – but don't count on that). Here is an interesting fact regarding the cost of living versus income during the decade between 2012-2022. Overall, the annual pay increased 3-5%, and the annual inflation rate never exceeded that level. However, if we carve out the short-term period that has included the national pandemic crisis, followed by incredibly high inflation, then the cost of living has significantly outpaced incomes. Dating back just three years, 2020-2022, median income has grown by 7% while overall cost has increased by 16%. One of the things consumers have done to combat the ever-stretching distance between income and cost has been to increase the usage of credit cards, exacerbating an already dire situation. American households seem to be taking a cue from the American government when it comes to overspending and creating mounds of debt. Google www.usdebtclock.org – there the debt clock provides a second -by- second accounting of the massive U.S. debt. On this date (January 16, 2023) that number is $31,492,627,400,800.00 – and moves faster than I can I record the numbers. As of this same date the U.S. is operating with a U.S. Budget Deficit of $1,527,479,555,823.00. If you are trying to count the zeroes, those numbers represent trillions of dollars in debt and overspending. Many American families are financially immobilized by debt, and that fact includes many Christians. Thus, the issue is not confined to our government and our own households, it cannot but trickle down and have a major (negative) impact on our churches. Every pastor and local church leadership should be ready to adopt any practical and Biblical means possible to assist their congregations to lift themselves from the cascading problem of debt. The church should be the first to throw a lifeline to their membership so that before they drown in a sea of debt.

THE DEFINITION OF DEBT

"Debt is a financial liability or obligation owed by one person, the debtor, to another, the creditor." It has been said that debt comes in many forms. Relative to our financial lives it tends to fall into one of the following categories: unsecured debt – which simply means that one's signature is the only requirement for the transaction; secured debt – obviously, this means that some form of collateral has been required in order for the transaction to be completed; revolving debt – open accounts, such as credit cards, and an open line of credit are included in this category, and may or may not be collateralized (such as a home equity line of credit); mortgage debt – the name is self-defining. A house is collateralized over an extended period with fifteen-to-thirty-year mortgage loans being the most typical real estate loans. Any of these transactional types constitute debt. Dating back to college days, I have long loved using a thesaurus. In sermon preparation it is always nearby. When I turn there to find the word debt the reference takes up one-third of the page in my copy of the thesaurus. Some of the synonyms given do not produce any warm, fuzzy feelings: deficit, default, liability, debtor, up against it, owing, in arrears, encumbered, running a tab...see what I mean? As always in a thesaurus, it provides a list of antonyms, and it says simply, "see payment." Yup, with debt there is always a payment. And, therein is the problem, too many payments.

When it comes to borrowing money – which is what we are doing with every credit-based purchase we make – we should ask ourselves a few questions.

First, why borrow? While this may sound like an almost silly question, I can state from experience it is not. Why do you think the average one-hour television show has between 14 and 18 minutes of commercials in the programming. What the eye sees, the heart wants! A 30-minute TV show has about 20 minutes of actual programing. There are entire networks who do nothing but promote products for consumers to buy. It can feel easy to buy now, pay later, and those impulse buying decisions can often come with great peril. I once counseled a husband and wife, both of whom were professionals, who had an issue with her addiction to a particular shopping network. "Stuff" would be delivered to their front door daily. I mean big boxes of stuff. I am not exaggerating when I say it was an addiction, and like most addictions her suppliers had no qualms about taking advantage of her addiction. Repeated attempts were made to have the sellers understand the problem and stop enabling her addiction. Those appeals went unheeded. All these type purchases tend to involve the use of a credit card. The clients to whom I referred were repeatedly taking funds from their retirement accounts to payoff large credit card balances.

Next comes the question, is there such a thing a good, or acceptable debt? To fully answer the question, let's back up and broaden our definition of debt. In our efforts to do that let's seek to better understand the actual cost of debt. Too many times I have had to talk clients off the cliff of some purchase that made little financial sense. Most of us have been tempted to make that kind of purchase. Marketing departments stay awake all night devising new ways to appeal to our emotions. We are captivated by those slick commercials that are always telling me I need what they are selling. A bigger, better, newer version of the newer whatchamacallit. The product doesn't really matter, it's the appeal that snags us. There is an entire chapter later in the book on the psychology of money. The point is we sometimes allow our emotions to gain the upper hand when making buying decisions. If we first stopped to count the actual cost of what we want to buy, we might make a different decision. Too often what the eye sees, the heart wants, and we make irrational buying decisions. Credit based purchases cost money....and in our current environment with rising interest rates there will be many people who find it more and more difficult to make those monthly payments. In March of 2022 the Federal Reserve reported that revolving credit rates – which includes credit cards – rose by more than 21%. Always look for alternatives to making credit purchases. Is there something that you already own that you could sell in order to make that purchase. Outside of buying a house, I had a little test that helped me a decide on using credit versus cash to make a purchase. Could my money earn more than the interest I would be charged for using the credit? The answer to that question is fluid, not static. Interest rates, inflation and market conditions all influence that decision. An extension of that first question is what will a loan cost me? We all know the adage, "time is money." But it is also true that time costs money. Both the cost to purchase an automobile and the cost to finance an auto loan have reached the teetering point. In 2015 the average price of a car across the U.S. was $35,294.00. By October 2022 that average price had reached $48,281.00, up from $40,107.00 in 2020. Checking bankrate.com we find that the interest rates for buying cars has also skyrocketed. Our point here is that buying that car has a cost, but there are many other costs associated with buying that vehicle. Bankrate.com predicts that new car loans will reach 6.9% by the end of 2023. In the first quarter of 2022 that rate was 4.07%. Sources indicate that nationally the typical down payment on an auto purchase is about 12%, so using the 2022 average price, a person would then finance $42,487.00. As I write this in January 2023 I can find, for those in the military, a rate of 4.74% for car purchases. Beyond that the rates seem to hover around 5.25%. Using that rate and the purchase price of $42,487.00 for a five-year auto loan will require a monthly payment of $806.66. That means paying the down payment of $5,794.72 plus the payments totaling $48,399.60 ($54,194.32). None of those numbers includes taxes and fees, nor the cost of operating, insuring, licensing, registration, and maintaining the car for the next sixty months. Bankrate.com states that the average cost across the U.S. to operate and maintain a new car in 2021 was $9,666.00.

Another question for our consideration is, "who is a debtor?" The obvious answer is anyone who owes money (or anything else) to anyone. True, but. What could possibly be the "but?" What if our definition of a debtor was anyone who owes for more they own. Many years ago, in a class lead by Ron Blue, he led a discussion around this very question. The basic answer became which is the bigger number – what we own or what we owe? Of course, that answer taken at face value could still get us into a financial mess, but it is a good starting point in answering the earlier question related to, is there debt that is not bad debt. The rationale around that statement rests in one's ability to liquidate all they own in order to fully pay off what they owe. That number resides on the bottom line of our personal net worth statement. Larry Burkett (Crown Financial) tended toward a hardline belief that one just needed to avoid debt. While I personally "hate" debt, I do think, that there are responsible ways to use debt as leverage to improve one's financial situation. Homebuyers will likely buy their first house with the use of a mortgage. Business owners often borrow to expand a business or improve operations. Credit is being afforded the opportunity to borrow money. When we exercise our credit and use borrowed money, we create a debt. Unless you know an incredibly generous lender, they all expect to be paid.

DANGER OF DEBT

Debt often extracts a high price. There is always the money factor, but it can also extract it's cost relative to our peace of mind (emotional well-being), our physical relationships and our spiritual relationships. Most wars are fought over issues of power and money. I have seen relational wars erupt over the same two factors.

There is most obviously the financial danger.... we have already provided much detail about the impact of reverse compounding in matters of debt. I use a credit card for almost any purchase I make.

Groceries, restaurants, gasoline, dry cleaning…you name it, I likely put it on a card. It's convenient, I earn rewards points (which I redeem) and it is free. I never carry a balance forward – so don't charge more than you are willing and capable of paying off. I think of my two cards, not as credit cards, but convenience cards. In fact, my American Express card is a charge-card. It has no set limit on what I can charge, and it has no installment options. The only option available to me is to pay it in full when I receive the statement. I like it that way! Just imagine you have a $3,000.00 balance on a credit card with an average rate of 17.5%. You want to get debt paid down so you decide to no longer make any charges on the card, and your goal is to pay off the balance in 36 months. Your monthly payments for the 36 months will be $184.00. You will have paid a total of $6,660.00 to eliminate that debt. The use of that $3,000.00 cost an additional $3,660.00. That sounds punitive, right? That's just one of the dangers of debt. Debt is dangerous on the spiritual level because it can be somewhat presumptive. The Bible (James 4:13-16) speaks to that problem. James is almost saying "how dare you think that you know what the future will bring." Yet, many of us live as if we will always make good money, get good pay increases, maintain good health, enjoy the benefits of a thriving economy, and on our way we go. James reminds us that life is fragile, even like a puff of smoke that appears and then quickly vanishes in the wind. The use of debt and making those payments presumes that everything will always be good and getting better. What will happen when our presumption is wrong? Surely the recent COVID pandemic taught us something. The use of debt could also be presumptuous in the fact that we were not willing to wait long enough to see how God might want to meet our needs in some fashion outside the realm of debt. Debt can also endanger our relationships. We guys are less reluctant to plunge ahead to use borrowed resources to buy (_you fill in the blank here_). Within the family, with a few exceptions, it is usually the wife who stresses out over the financial management decisions of the family. That stress impacts physical and psychological health. So yes, there is the pecuniary danger associated with debt, there is certainly the psychological dangers associated with debt, and if not careful in the use of debt can bring great personal danger and damage our way. Currently, the best possible credit score in America is 850. Only about 1.2% of the population have that score. In 2021 the average score across all American was 714 – a 4-point increase from 2020. It comes as no surprise that the highest average score (760) comes in the age 76+ segment. It ranges down to an average score of just under 679 found in the age 18-24 population. In 2021 30% of the population had a "Subprime" credit score (580-669). It is estimated that about 11% of the population is "credit invisible," that is little or nothing showing in the credit files. I include these statistics only to validate the possibility of damaging our personal reputation by neglecting sound financial management principles in our personal and business lives.

DESTROYING DEBT

Dan Aykroyd was instrumental in the creation of a movie that became so much more than a move – it become a cultural phenomenon. In June 1984 the movie Ghost Busters hit the screens and found immediate success. The accompanying song, by the same name had several verses, one of which said, *"Don't get caught up alone oh, no – Ghostbusters! - when it comes through your door, unless you want some more, I think you better call Ghostbusters!"* By now I hope that I have persuaded you that lingering debt is something more horrifying than any notion of a ghost. But, just as those lyrics suggest, you don't have to do face the monster called debt alone, there is help on the way and before it can get worse, act. It's time that we decide to become debt busters.

In churches and communities across America financial teaching is taking place that can enable Christians to become debt free and to learn sound concepts that can both destroy debt, but also heal the pain often associated with financial stress. For many years I facilitated Crown Financial Ministries groups in churches, including my own. Our church has also successfully used the Financial Peace University materials. No matter the format or formula we might use to destroy debt it must begin with a decision, which must then be followed by a dogged determination to win this battle. For couples the battle cannot be won without the full engagement of wife and husband. I intentionally listed the wife first in the previous sentence. Sorry guys, but my experience has been that our wives are a lot smarter than us on so many financial decisions. It will take wife, husband and Holy Spirit to win this war. If there is a struggle making ends meet it is likely that you bought what you could not afford and borrowed what you struggle to repay.

I don't mean to oversimplify the process – it can be hard – but here are a few basic steps to get started on becoming a debt-buster:

- Commitment – ask God to provide guidance and enablement on this journey. The same God who saved you by allowing His Son to die on a cross for your sins is interested in saving you from financial struggle. Make God part of your financial plan. Ask him to create discipline and determination in your spirit.
- Calculate – create a list of your assets (things you own or have equity in), then create a list of all that you owe (don't leave anything out). Now the dreaded part, prepare a budget. Account for each source of income and list every expense. Don't forget those taxes, things such as auto registrations and maintenance, Christmas and birthdays, trips, lunch money.....write it all down.
- Change – here comes the work. Something must change. Limit credit card spending. If discipline is an issue, it could be time to cut up those credit cards. There is the matter of living within your means – the budget is just that, a budget is a spending plan. If there is no current margin in your budget for savings that will become one of your first goals – pay down debt and begin saving toward a cash reserve. Remember, the culprit is not the card. The culprit is failing to pay off the balance each month on the card and paying outsized interest charges on those balances. Again, if you cannot exercise the discipline of limited spending and paying off the monthly balance on credit cards, then charge cards may not be right for you.

- Cascade – a simple way to begin paying down balances is to begin with the smallest balance and do all within your ability to pay it off as soon as possible. Direct any "free" cash flow to that account. Once paid, move to the second credit account on your list – continue to pay what you have been paying on this second account, but now add to that amount the money that you were paying on the first account (which has now been paid in full). When the second account is paid, move to the third. Take all you were paying on the second account and add to what you had been paying on the third account. Continue this cascading, or snowballing, effect until all that debt is gone.
- Contentment – advertising is designed to make you want something you do not currently have. I've heard people say, "I'm just going over to walk around through the mall." When did that ever happen? Marketing is designed to appeal to both needs and wants. We Americans have huge appetites that extend well beyond our needs. I'm not suggesting a monastic life for us, but my experience has taught me that most of us have a great deal to learn about contentment. In Philippians 4:11 the Apostle Paul said, "...*I have learned in whatever situation I am to be content...*" Note, he learned that it did not come naturally. Pray and ask God to help you and to show you what that means.

In summary, we could think of debt in this way:

- Debt can be punitive – the Bible indicates it can make us prisoners.
- Debt can be presumptuous – we might be missing out on what God wants to show us and do for us in terms of financial security.
- Debt can be provocative – our desires and assumptions are often enticed by alluring advertising that makes buying now and paying later attractive.

- Debt can be pernicious in its effect - pernicious is defined as harmful in a gradual or subtle way. That sounds about right, don't you agree?

It is likely that our personal peace of mind and financial well-being has no more serious enemy that indebtedness. With some drowning in debt, some struggling to stay afloat, I pray this book will serve as a lifeline of hope. May we not simply survive, may we thrive and "*...renew our strength...mount up with wings like eagles....not be weary....and not faint.*" (Isaiah 40:31)

CHAPTER 5
The Provision: God the Provider

I alluded to it in our last chapter when I stated that the use of extensive debt can be somewhat presumptuous on our part. Could our rush to buy on credit – whatever the purchase is – be ignoring the provision of God and his promise to, as Paul said it, *"supply every need of yours according to his riches in glory in Christ Jesus."* (Phil. 4:19) Can we not trust God? Do we pray about our buying decisions? Are we willing to wait on God? His storehouse never has a shortage, let's learn to trust Him more.

In our Western culture a person's name is basically just a way of identifying a person. Today parents chose a name because it is pretty, or popular, or has a nice sound, or it might honor a special friend or relative. As often as not it becomes a matter of searching through the various books that contain endless lists of names. In the Eastern world, especially in Bible times, there was meaning and purpose in the selection of a name. A name was regarded as expressing a deep desire of the parent's heart, or it might have even given a clue as to the character of the child. An example of this is found when Rachel gave birth to Benjamin. She named him Benoni, "son of my sorrow." For Rachel this was an expression of her life experiences.

Even the most casual reader of the Bible recognizes the many names and titles given to God in scripture. In the Bible there are three primary names for God:

Elohim.......God
Adonai......Lord
Jehovah....LORD, GOD
Beyond this there are three secondary names for God:
El Shaddai......Almighty God
El Elyon..........Most High God
El Olam..........Everlasting God

Then there are nine names compounded with the name Jehovah. Each of those names teaches us something about the nature and work of God in and through our lives.

JEHOVAH-JIREH

The intent of this chapter is to focus only on one of those names, and that is Jehovah-Jireh. Turning our attention to Genesis 22 we find the account of Abraham receiving instruction from God to travel to the region of Moriah for the purpose of making a sacrifice. No problem we might think, for Abraham was a wealthy man and could afford anything the Lord might ask of him. But ah, it was Abraham's son Isaac, the son for whom he had longed, waited, and prayed, who would be the sacrifice. Now the Lord would require the life of that precious boy. In Genesis we find Abraham making that trek to Moriah, up to the mountain to prepare the altar of sacrifice. See him as he takes Isaac and is prepared to offer him up to God when at the last God intervenes and gives Abraham a substitute sacrifice. In Genesis 22:14 we find these words, *"So Abraham called that place The Lord will Provide. And to this day it is said, "On the mountain the Lord will provide."* Did you see it? There it was, Jehovah-Jireh! The Lord will provide." That is what the name means...**the Lord will provide!**

Jireh in Hebrew is a form of the verb "to see." In most of the places it occurs it is translated "to see or to appear." Why then is it translated "provide" in Genesis 22? Provide is the verb form of "seeing beforehand" and prevision is the noun of "seeing beforehand." Thus, with God prevision is always followed by provision. The God who sees beforehand is the God who provides. Therefore, to say, "the Lord will provide" is the same as saying "the Lord will see to it." The Lord wonderfully provides for his people.

ABUNDANT PROVISIONS

SACRIFICE FOR OUR SINS

In reflecting on Abraham's story in the Genesis passage we see that the provisions of God focused on a sacrifice and a substitute. The history of Abraham was marked by four great crises, each a test of his faith and each involved the surrender of something that was very dear to him. First, he was called on to separate himself from his native land. (Genesis 12) Next, he was called on to leave his nephew Lot behind when they parted ways. (Genesis 13) He was then called on to abandon his plan concerning Ishmael. (Genesis 17) The supreme test then came when God asked for Isaac. (Genesis 22) Like the life of Abraham, the Christian life is a series of experiences which often test our faith. Only by discipline can there be any growth and development in our faith life. In Genesis 22:8 we read Abraham's statement of faith, "God shall provide..." What God provided in that instance was a ram which served as a substitute on the altar, thus sparing the life of Isaac. This of course is a perfect picture of the sacrifice that Jesus Christ made for us at Calvary when he, the innocent Lamb of God, died for our sin. On Moriah Abraham received a gospel message that declares we don't have to die, for God has provided the lamb for the offering.

COUNSEL FOR OUR CRISIS

God's abundant provision also includes coming to us in the many instances of uncertainty, trouble, and despair in our lives and providing a sense of guidance, direction, and peace. No matter our crisis, God provides the wisdom and counsel we need. Proverbs 3:5-6 says, *"Trust in the Lord with all your heart and lean not on your own understanding; in all your ways acknowledge him and will make your paths straight."* (NIV) The Psalmist declared, *"Thou shalt guide me with thy counsel..."* (Psalm 73:24) God can counsel us from the divine perspective considering His infinite wisdom. Therefore, we need to stop trusting in ourselves and begin consulting God for His wisdom. Whether we are talking about a financial crisis or any other crisis, God has provided a divine, inspired Word for us.

SPIRIT TO SUSTAIN US

In John's gospel (chapter 14) we find the disciples disturbed and confused by all the talk about the death and departure of Jesus. During their concern, Jesus announced that they would not be left comfortless or left as orphans with no one to care for them, but rather a provision had been made on their behalf. The Holy Spirit was being provided them to be their companion and sustainer. God's provision for His people is that we never have to be separated from Him because of the presence of the Spirit. Why don't you stop right now and invite the Holy Spirit into your financial life? I can promise you, if you do, He will show up. And, you know what.... His ideas are better than yours.

ABSOLUTE ABUNDANCE

Do you feel as though you are living in a time of abundance? Or do you seem to always be just a little short, or you wish there was just a little extra so that you could do this or that? We need to know that any shortages that we may be experiencing, any lack of abundance, is not God's fault, but rather man's fault. In Philippians 4:19 the Bible states, *"And my God will meet all your needs according to his glorious riches in Christ Jesus."* (NIV) God stands willing, able, and ready to provide all that I need, nothing withstanding. Any shortage of resources in our lives is because we have short circuited the plan of God along the way, and most often that means we have violated the principles of God that relate to money. There may be a few exceptions, but most often our own disobedience, our running ahead of God, is the thing that created the financial need in our life.

Take note of the fact that God is prepared to provide for us not out of His riches, but according to His riches. What are these riches? First, in Psalms 24:1, the Bible says, *"The earth is the Lord's, and everything in it, the world, and all who live in it."* So, it's all His. Look around you! Look up! What do you see? It's all His. God owns it all, all that you see are part of his riches. The Bible also says in Psalms 50:10, *"For every animal of the forest is mine, and the cattle on a thousand hills."* Every living thing belongs to God and is under His command and in His control. Just as surely as he sent a bird to feed Elijah the prophet, God will use all at His disposal to provide for our needs today. In Haggai 2:8 God declares, *"The silver is mine and the gold is mine..."* Wall Street, Fort Knox, the Federal Reserve, and the Fortune 500 pale in comparison to the riches of our God. With God there is no danger of a stock market correction, no chance of bankruptcy or bank failure, no prospect of a depression. His treasury is inexhaustible, and He promises to meet our needs according to this unlimited supply. How sad and tragic that so many of us will never trust God enough to test His resources. With God there is an absolute abundance. Jesus said in John 10:10, *"...I have come that they may have life and have it to the full."* We will return to this topic of God's abundance in a later chapter. Yes, God is our provider.... but, do you believe that statement? Do you operate as though that statement is true? The Bible makes that certain declaration over and over. What is lacking in your life? Many will immediately think of something in the financial realm, and that's okay. However, the assurance of God to meet all our needs extends well beyond finances. How about your children and family? How about your health? How about your marriage? What facet of your life feels as though there are current shortages? We marvel at the stories of God's miraculous intervention throughout the Bible, but we often live as though those times have past, and that God has taken a sabbatical from miracles and divine intervention in our lives. He has no shortages, and His supply room is open to any believer who approaches Him in open and honest faith. You are a child of the King, stop living like beggars.

CHAPTER 6

The Psychology: Lessons from Behavioral Science

Once, in a group setting being led by Ron Blue, the question was asked, "How much is enough? How would you answer that question. Before you answer the question ponder this thought....money can be a tool, or a tyrant. Money can be a tool to improve one's life, to bless our families, advance the Kingdom of God, improve our communities and plan our future. However, if we are not careful (biblically centered), money can become a tyrant, demanding more and more of our time, our attention, and become our master. John D. Rockefeller, at the height of his wealth, owned 90% of all the oil and gas industry in the U.S. His personal net worth equaled about 1% of the entire U.S. economy. When asked how much money is enough, he replied, "just a little bit more." What drives an incredibly successful and rich business tycoon to think and behave so as to always want to have a little bit more? What makes a wealthy and successful businessman like Bernie Madoff decide to create a fraudulent investment scheme? In legitimate business transactions his firm traded over $740 million per day. Per day! He was hugely and legitimately successful. Why then would Madoff, with all his wealth, be so desperate for more money that he would criminally bilk millions from friends and clients in a Ponzi scheme? All for just a little bit more. We ask, what were they thinking?

That is why this chapter on the psychology of money belongs in this book.

THE MILLIONAIRE NEXT DOOR

I cannot begin to remember who introduced me to the book titled "The Millionaire Next Door." I do know that it made an immediate impact on my life and continues to even to this very day. Authors Tomas Stanley and William Danko emphatically state that millionaires are disproportionately living in middle-class and blue-collar neighborhoods, not in what most judge to be affluent and wealthy neighborhoods. A different author refers to what he calls," wealth that you don't see." The premise of both statements is that often the appearance of wealth and status is merely a game of shadows. Our judgments are often formed by what we see. I have for many years, as a financial planner, been privy to the personal financial affairs of a great many people. I can attest to the truth of Stanley and Danko's book. Looks can be deceiving. As Morgan Housel says, "Someone driving a $100,000 car might be wealthy. But the only data point you have about their wealth is that they have $100,000 less than they did before they bought the car, or $100,000 more in debt." In America, according to Stanley and Danko, the reality is that many high-income earners are UAW's (under accumulator of wealth) – that is they save a little and spend a lot. On the other hand, there are the PAW's (prodigious accumulator of wealth). These individuals tend to live well below their means and place great value on saving and investing. Their choices in cars, houses and clothes may seldom match their true net worth. In other words some lifestyles fall into the category of "better than." In other words, their consumptive lifestyle gives the appearance of doing "better than" their incomes can sustain. Another tendency discovered among those living affluent lifestyles is that many individuals are operating under the "better off" philosophy. Those persons come from modest backgrounds – now find themselves in financially successful careers – and determine they can live "better off" than they did growing up. Don't you see, all of this is intertwined with the psychology of money. Just be sure of this – your eventual financial wellbeing is much more about your savings habits more than anything else. Furthermore, once one reaches a certain level of income, Housel says what you need is "just what sits below your ego."

IRRATIONAL BEHAVIOR

While a graduate student at the University of Alabama I took an elective course from the course offerings within the financial planning degree program. The course appeared in the catalog as CSM 535 – The Psychology of Money. Perhaps I opted for the class because I found its title appealing, and it certainly was. Or perhaps it was the teachers name – Eve Pentecost – that captured my attention. Surely you can understand why a preacher/financial planner would be hooked on both the name of the course and the name of the teacher. She was a terrific teacher, and the course did not disappoint. As she and I eventually determined, we were distant kinfolks (my Mom's sister married a Pentecost). However, there was an outside required reading list that contained one book that I was not looking forward to reading. The title was *Predictably Irrational,* by Dan Ariely. While the name was not put-offish, the author was. Upon reading his bio and learning that he was an economist, my initial reaction was one of dread, accompanied by the almost certainty of absolute boredom. Wow, I was wonderfully surprised. What he had to say was not only entertaining and enjoyable, but the insights he provided into the human psychology of decision making relative to money were eye opening. Ariely believes that a greater understanding of behavioral economics provides the basis for consumer science, which in part focuses on our consumer decisions, why we make those decisions, and the impact of that decision on both individuals and society. His book reinforces the idea that many of our financial decisions are clouded by irrational behavior. Most people would say, and believe, that most of their financial decisions are well informed and intelligent decisions. Ariely convinced me that most of us are predictably irrational in our choices. Our economic behavior, though most often irrational, is in fact predictable. If that statement is factual, and I believe it is, who else do you think understands the concept? Sure – the people who set public policy, the people who design advertising campaigns, the folks who ask for donations and contributions – all of them want something you have and if they take the time to study human behavior, they have the key to influencing our spending and saving choices.

CONFLICTS AND MONEY

As I write, multiple times throughout the day, the ever-talking media hosts keep reminding us that our nation – positioned against Russia, China and North Korea – could be on the verge of war. Russia has been in a hostile war with the Ukraine for month after month. Such thoughts are sobering. But I also contend that as Christians we are watching the attempts at a hostile takeover of our culture – it will come down to the church versus culture – that is also a war. Yet, it is behind the closed doors of thousands of families that another conflict is brewing, in fact, already a war for some. In our homes and families, it is often conflict and hostility relative to money that is ticking away like a bomb. I've counseled couples who feel – and on paper it is true – that their money woes are never ending. It is more than living from paycheck to paycheck...that would be an improvement...drowning in the steady drip of financial demands on their lives. From a psychological perspective it could be that we are not addressing the real issue in our conversations with couples who live under constant stress related to money. Yes, money and the lack thereof are a problem. At the heart of the issue, it could be something that lies just below the surface, it could be an issue of values and the behaviors that stem from those values. I would coach any couple having repeated arguments about money to momentarily step back from the money issue and spend time discussing – in a calm manner – what money really means to each of you, and what the role of money in your life means. One of you may feel strongly that money is linked to feelings of security and stability, while one of you feels that money is meant to be enjoyed to its fullest – have fun, take an extended vacation, buy the latest gadgets. Neither feeling is wrong, it is simply that they tend to be at opposite ends of the financial spectrum. Try taking time to write down three or four things you each value relative to money. Then attach a financial goal to that value. Review the section in this book about goal setting. Does each value support a particular goal? Compare your lists. Now for the hard stuff...jointly agree on what you really want to put on your list of financial goals, and prioritize them. Don't rush this process. For each of you, what habits or behaviors fail to align with your values supported goals? We can all develop habits that sabotage our desired outcomes. Be caringly honest with each other as you assess what financial habits and tendencies each has that do not truly support your goals. It is here that you must create a plan – including a budget – and set in motion the actions that lead to a sense of mutual accomplishment. The final chapter in this book is about creating accountability for your personal success. I strongly suggest that couples work with someone outside the immediate family who can serve as that accountability partner. It could be a trusted friend at church, or it could be a financial planner. To borrow an old advertising slogan from Nike, "Just Do It! Money can be a huge stressor that can lead to negative feelings of dread and despondency, feelings of entrapment...not to mention what stress does to the human body. On the extreme side of money related mental health issues research has indicated that overwhelming financial issues can lead to depression, alcohol dependency, drug dependency and other psychotic issues. It is not uncommon to see chronic pain and other physical symptoms manifest during times of financial duress.

On the other side of this topic there is research to support a few conclusions we might make about money and happiness. In 2010 psychologist Dan Kahneman and economist Angus Deaton teamed up in a research project about the possible link between money and happiness. Among the notable findings in the project was that they found that levels of happiness increased with income until income was sufficient to meet basic needs and a few luxuries. After that point, money did not typically equate to more happiness. In the study it was reported that the ideal income for optimal happiness was about $75,000.00 (adjusted +/- for regional costs). I should point out that the study defined happiness through words such as contentment, pride, amusement, compassion, love and other such terms. It is also worth noting that the higher wage earners most often expressed self-oriented emotions while lower wage earners more often expressed other-oriented emotions, such as love and compassion.

MONEY GENOGRAM

One of the assignments given we grad students in the course on the psychology of money was to complete a money genogram. My keen interest in my family tree has me rummaging through old records, roaming (physically and virtually) through church cemeteries, chasing down distant kinfolk... all in an effort to learn more about my roots. A Money Genogram is like a family tree that depicts family behaviors, attitudes and beliefs about money. Our financial mindset, and consequently our behaviors, are derived from the things that were consciously and unconsciously taught – and what we observed from our family – dating back to our early childhood. The purpose of completing the genogram is not about right or wrong, instead, it is a tool to help us understand our use of, and our feelings about money. Each one of us has a different money story, and understanding that story could help us affirm that certain things we are doing are "spot-on." Yet, it could also help us re-invent ourselves in certain matters related to money. I encourage you to find the article titled "Your Money Story," which can be found at foothill.edu and develop your family money genogram. More on the subject can be found at hartfordfunds.com. I encourage you – and if married – both of you, to spend time creating and analyzing your own money story. As needed, may the truth set you free.

MONEY HAS PERSONALITY

No, not really. Money is neutral, it has no personality, but we humans who use money have plenty of personality, don't we? In my book *CHOSEN,* in which I describe the personality of the disciples chosen by Jesus to follow him, I explain some of the theories of human personality types, and the tools often used to identify those types. Such information is important in understanding the how and why of what we do, and how we relate to others and the situations that surround us. This book takes that information and uses it to seek a greater understanding of how we relate to money and the decisions we make about and toward money. So, while money has no personality of its own, it can take on the personality of the person spending, seeking or saving the money.

As Christians, in order to gain a broader understanding of our management of our God owned (and entrusted to us) resources, let's take a step back to the Garden of Eden. I completed my undergraduate degree the University of Mobile, which has built a rich tradition around the Latin phrase, *Imago Dei,* "the image of God." It speaks to the fact that human beings are set apart from every other creature on earth. As dysfunctional as we can seem and act at times, we remain amazingly remarkable – almost divine, wouldn't you say? God created us in His image, placed us in Eden, and then gave us the assignment of responsibly managing God's creation and all its glorious resources, and today that includes money. It is interesting to note that so long as Adam and Eve properly managed God's resources they lived surrounded by peace and prosperity. Yet, the moment they botched the assignment, chaos ensued. We humans remain caught up in a chaotic, broken system to this very moment. Oh, we catch glimpses of what it was and what it could be, but somehow our freewill keeps injecting itself- in unhealthy ways – into our relationships with God, family, friends and our interactions and transactions that touch God's creation. It is within this thought that our unique personalities come to light as we mingle and comingle with people and the resources which compose all that God originally put in Eden.

In a 2021 CNBC report, based on the work of author Ken Honda, there are supposedly seven distinct money personality types. It should be remembered, as I stated in CHOSEN, that in matters of personality and our interactions with others (and in this case money), we are all to some degree a composite of types. In the psychology of personality, we have a dominate style, overlapped by other styles. Under pressure, or as we often say, "when backed into a corner," we will revert to our dominate style. The CNBC report includes these seven styles:

- Compulsive savers – frugal, views money as security, saves before spending.
- Compulsive spenders – spends to relieve stress, makes unnecessary purchases, seeks immediate gratification.
- Compulsive moneymaker – top priority in life is to always make more money, seeks recognition of others.

- Indifferent – rarely thinks about money, tends to be well-off financially.
- Saving / Splurging – vacillates between the two, tends to be impulsive
- Gambler – takes big risks with money, in certain ways is a blend of the spender and moneymaker.
- Worrier – always worried about money, may lack confidence in their own ability to become financially independent.

It is incumbent on us that we recognize that we have developed, at least in part, our attitudes and affinity for (or lack of) money from our relationships. That includes parents and extended families, our friends and certainly our workmates – and our economic environment. What we sometimes fail to remember is that God wants us to allow Him to weave the tapestry our life story to include His image, and all our healthy surroundings.

Tommy Brown has written a book, *The Seven Money Types,* which bears the subtitle, "Discover how God wired you to handle money." He takes seven characters, all from the Old Testament, and uses their relationship with money and resources to define how each of them reflects the characteristics of the image of God. As I pointed out earlier in my own research, with each type comes the potential for flaws, which Brown refers to as one's "shadow side." I close this chapter with a quote from Brown's book, "Now I've discovered the key to financial well-being is to stop striving for what you do not have and to reach into who you are, into who God designed you to be, and to start your journey there."

CHAPTER 7
The Principles: Money and the Bible

From my years in the ministry as a pastor I remember most vividly an annual event in the church, typically in the late fall, which had been preceded by the preparation of the church budget, known as Stewardship Emphasis. What that really meant is that I had to prepare a month's supply of sermons on the "M" word. Money! The congregation expected it, and frankly needed it, but never enjoyed it. It was just one of those things that one had to endure, sort of the dues for belonging. As the pastor I would always cringe just a bit when I would walk onto the platform on Sunday morning and see a guest in the audience, or see those that I had invited for quite some time and of all times for them to make good on their months of promises to attend, they picked the very day I was to preach on the "M" word. I could just hear what they were going to say as they left church that day. They would surely say, "I knew it, that's all those preachers ever talk about… money, money, money. That's all they want; they just want your money."

In Christian circles we at times are reluctant to talk about money. Perhaps we think it's too secular a subject. Leave such talk to the business world. Why, we're much to pious to concern ourselves with such worldly, mundane talk. We have lofty spiritual matters that demand our attention. We have theology to debate, meetings to plan, Bible classes to teach, souls to save. Mind you, I am not intending to make light of that which is vital to the mission of the church. What I am suggesting is that many a Christian has allowed their testimony, and therefore their effectiveness for God, to be damaged and destroyed because they neglected and abused their financial affairs.

THE BIBLE SPEAKS

Pick a topic, any topic related to spiritual and religious life. How about prayer? Evangelism? What about heaven or hell? Or the ever popular second coming of Christ. How about grace or the second birth? What topic do you suppose is given the most coverage in the Bible? If you guessed money, then you are right. That's right, money. There are more than 700 direct references to money in the Bible. Jesus had more to say about money than any other subject. In fact, two thirds of the parables deal with the use of money. Since the Bible has so much to say about money, we Christians must listen. If we expect to receive the blessings of God, then we must discover, and then live by His principles for mastering and managing money. Money and its influences can have a powerful and lasting impact on our lives. We are responsible and accountable to God for how money impacts our lives and how we use money to impact others. Christians often talk about stewardship. (Which we discuss fully in another chapter) The Greek word translated stewardship is most often "oikonomia." It refers to the management of property which belongs to another, such as we see in Luke 16:2-4. Jesus related the words of the owner in that parable, *"What is this I hear about you? Give an account of your management because you cannot be manager any longer."* Psalm 8:6 says, *"You made him ruler over the works of your hands; you put everything under his feet."* There is no escaping our responsibility regarding money. For that reason, we need to search the Bible and learn all that God has given us for instruction about money and how to master money so that we might live financially free.

THE PRINCIPLE OF POSSESSIONS

To have a true understanding of the Biblical perspective on money and resources it is necessary that we agree on the principle of ownership. Most Christians would be quick to agree that yes, God owns everything, which in fact He does. You and I own nothing. We may have possessions that have been entrusted to us by God, but we own nothing. My role as one who has possessions but owns nothing is one of having no rights but having a great responsibility to properly manage what has been entrusted to me.

David clearly understood this principle:

"Yours, O Lord, is the kingdom; you are exalted head overall. Wealth and honor come from you; you are the ruler of all things." (I Chronicles 29:11,12 NIV)

The gospel of John tells us why God has the right to claim ownership to absolutely everything:

"Through him all things were made; without him nothing was made that has been made." John 1:3 NIV

The basic reason that individuals are so busy and in such a rush to possess things is to fulfill a need for a sense of security. We think, somehow, that if we can just surround ourselves with enough things and enough money then we will not only feel good about ourselves, but we will also feel secure. Such thinking is distorted, for real security cannot be bought with any amount of money but is found through a personal relationship with Jesus Christ.

To illustrate that point we find in Luke 12:16-21 a parable told by Jesus to a group of listeners. In the story the man has been very successful, and his business has grown and grown. In fact, business has been so good that the man finds that his resources have outgrown his ability to store all the abundance. So, he decides to build bigger and better facilities which will of course allow him to become even more successful and wealthy. In the parable the man looks at all that he seems to have accomplished and says:

"You have plenty of good things laid up for many years. Take life easy; eat, drink, and be merry."

Sounds like the good life, huh? Listen to the teaching of Jesus in response to this philosophy:

"You fool! This very night your life will be demanded from you. Then who will get what you have prepared for yourself?"

Jesus went on to say that this is how it will be with anyone who stores up things for himself but is not rich toward God. It should be seen therefore, that security is not found in what we possess, but in our relationship to God. God owns everything and simply allows us to enjoy the benefits associated with using what he owns. Once we really believe this principle, we are on our way to financial freedom.

As regards to our relationship with God and toward money, so much is directly linked to our personal attitude about possessions. No matter how much fervor and energy we might put into our relationship with God and our activities for the church, if our philosophy and attitude about money is wrong, then our relationship with God cannot be right. No amount of devotion or activity can overcome an improper or unbalanced attitude about money.

Jesus stated it succinctly in Matthew 6:24:

"No one can serve two masters. Either he will hate the one and love the other, or he will be devoted to the one and despise the other. You cannot serve God and money."

All too often Christians have sought to have a strong, viable relationship with God, while maintaining attachments to this world. James describes this desire by some in this way:

"...don't you know that friendship with the world is hatred toward God? Anyone who chooses to be a friend of the world becomes an enemy of God." (James 4:4)

Let's admit it. Money is a master! Nothing can influence people, even entire nations, like money. We are persuaded by it. We are empowered by it. We are motivated by it. We are impressed by it. Some will steal for it. Others even dare to kill for it. It is a master that can and does enslave.

Mind you, money in and of itself is not evil. Money is not in any way immoral. In fact, it is amoral, neither good nor bad. Rather it is our attitude regarding money that determines who and what it is that we really serve. Do you really want to find out what one's character is really like? Then don't send him into poverty, but suddenly give him wealth. The wealth will be a mirror giving an honest reflection of that individuals basic character.

Jesus has said that it is impossible to serve two masters, no matter how hard we might try. Sooner or later, we are going to show partiality to one or the other. If we become a slave to things, to money, to possessions, then we have ceased serving God. Our affection is set on what this life has to offer rather than what our relationship to God has to offer. Our seemingly endless quest for the "good life" has caused much of our nation to become plagued with materialism which is the very antitheses of spirituality. Look around! There can be no question, many have given money the place in their life that should be occupied by God. Our relationship to God is no stronger than our attitude about money. A right attitude results in a growing relationship to God, whereas a wrong attitude ensures a less than optimum relationship with God. In 1 John 2:15 we are told:

"Love not the world or anything in the world.
If anyone loves the world, the love of the
Father is not in him."

The systems of this world are opposed to God and the believer cannot afford to cling to this world, for the tighter our grip on this world, the less interest we are likely to have for spiritual matters. Make no mistake, there is a direct correlation between our affection for God and our attachment to money.

THE PRINCIPLE OF PROSPERITY

My grandmother Johnston was a born worrier. She worried about Grandpa, she worried about her children, she worried about we grandchildren, she worried about the weather, she worried about what to wear, she worried about what to cook, she worried about company coming, she worried about company not coming. In fact, if life was going really, really good, she worried because there was nothing to worry about. She is in heaven now with Grandpa, but the last time I saw her alive she was worried that I wasn't eating right, and I was over forty years of age at the time! Grandmother of course wanted nothing but the best for all of us, and we often kidded her about her worrisome attitude. Unfortunately, there are some individuals in life who allow worry to totally control their life and rob them of happiness. They know little of the joy of worry-free living. Paul said in Philippians 4:6:

"Do not be anxious about anything."

I know, you're thinking Paul just had no idea what your life was going to be like. Really? In one of his letters to the Corinthian Church he described some of "bad" times in his life. No, he just had no idea how bad life could really be. That's why in 2 Corinthians 11 he described being imprisoned numerous times, flogged repeatedly, run out of town, stoned, shipwrecked, and lost at sea, exposed to cold winters with inadequate clothing, mugged and left for dead. So yes, Paul had doubts, distractions, detractors, disasters and near death experiences. Yet, he could still talk about contentment and having no anxieties. For Paul, he could say, *"I count everything as loss because of the surpassing worth of knowing Christ Jesus my Lord.* (Philippians 3:8)

Perhaps someone had shared with Paul the words of Jesus found in Matthew 6:25:

Therefore, I tell you, do not worry about your life,
What you will eat or drink, or about your body,
What you will wear. Is not life more important than
Food, and the body more important than clothes?

God has assigned a glorious purpose to all our lives and therefore is not going to allow us to go lacking. David said he had never seen the righteous forsaken or God's children begging bread. Anxiety can only sap our strength and our fretting can only serve to further frustrate us and certainly brings no resolution to any problem we might face. Make no mistake, our God is a God of abundance, and the gospel we preach and believe is a gospel of abundance and prosperity, but not to be confused with the so-call "prosperity gospel" we hear today.

Jesus turned to nature to illustrate how perfectly God takes care of all his creation. The birds of the air afforded Jesus an object lesson for his listeners. The birds, which had no ability to sow or reap or store produce, were provided for in every possible way. Is it not then reasonable to believe that man, created superior to all other creation and in the image of God Himself, will likewise be cared for by the Creator Himself?

Elizabeth Cheney wrote:
"Said the robin to the sparrow,
I should really like to know
Why these anxious human beings
Rush around and worry so.
Said the sparrow to the robin,
I think surely it must be
That they have no Heavenly Father
Such as cares for you and me."

We do of course have a Heavenly Father who has all the necessary resources to meet our every need. All of material structure, with man at the center, is arranged so as to graciously provide for man. Jesus asked the rhetorical question, *"Who of you by worrying can add a single hour to his life?"* At the heart of worry-free living must be a deep-seated belief that not only did God create this world and all that is in it, but it is also God who controls it all and keeps it all together. Paul stated it this way in Colossians 1:16-17.

"For by him all things were created: things in heaven and on earth, visible and invisible, whether thrones or powers or rulers or authorities; all things were created by Him and for Him. He is before all things, and in Him all things hold together."

Jesus is telling us that worry expresses a lack of faith in the ability of God to properly care for us. Can we not trust the willingness of God to provide for us? Someone has suggested that anxiety over these provisions is akin to the practice of practical atheism. No matter how we seek to dignify worry by giving it some other name (concern, burden, etc.) it is still sinful, and the results are always the same. The Greek word translated "take no thought" means "to be drawn in different directions." Worry pulls us apart as we seek to live our life dependent on material things and money. It is our own lack of faith that prevents God from working in our lives as He would. Worry free living is possible only when our focus is the Creator and Sustainer of all of life.

Perhaps worry-free living is best summarized in three simple thoughts found in Matthew chapter six.

Verse 30- FAITH- We must learn to trust God.

Verse 32- FATHER- Know that God cares.

Verse 33- FIRST- Always put God first.

Success is defined by some as "the achievement of a desired goal, such as obtaining a name and fame, or wealth, or a higher degree, for which a person has tried his level best." "The accomplishment of an aim or purpose". Biblically, do you see anything that might not align with God's perspective? There is nothing wrong with success, and who doesn't want to be successful? Just consider that God's standards for evaluating success may not always be congruent with our definition and standards. The Bible is filled with all sorts of noble, God-fearing folks. Financially, some of them were poor – like the widow who gave her small offering (Luke 21), - others were of modest means and worked hard (Nehemiah 4), - and others were wealthy (1 Chronicles 29). Yet, God's evaluation of them had nothing to do with their financial statement. To the prophet Samuel God said, *"Do not look at his appearance....for the Lord sees not as man sees; man looks on the outward appearance, but the Lord looks on the heart."* God is looking for a seeking heart! That is, a person who first and foremost, has become what I once heard called a "God-chaser." The Psalmist best defines who and what a God-chaser is, *"As a deer longs for a stream of cool water, so I long for you, O God. When can I go and worship in your presence?"* (Psalm 42:1-2 GNT) This was written by David at a low point in his life, a time of exile, a time of running and hiding. Clearly, he wasn't thinking about wealth...he was thinking about God. Yet, he was very wealthy. His perspective was God first, then all else follows.

THE PRINCIPLE OF PRIORITIES

In Matthew 6:19, 33 we find mention of two areas that demand we set priorities. In these two verses Jesus talks about our treasures and our thoughts, both of which have a great influence on how we live and how we relate to God.

Begin by looking at verse thirty-three, we are told, *"Seek first His kingdom and His righteousness, and all these things will be given unto you."* Of major consequence is the word seek. We all seek certain things in life. We seek happiness, we seek to belong, we seek to be successful, we seek material gain, we seek an education, we seek health, we seek acceptance, we seek love. I remember in my psychology classes that we studied Abraham Maslow's hierarchy of needs. His theory states that we are all in search of some of the same things. He put them in pyramid form with the basic needs of life laid as the foundation of the pyramid: physiological needs such as food, shelter and clothing; safety needs, including personal security, employment, health and property; the need to belong and be loved, to include family and friends; needs like respect, self-esteem status, recognition and freedom are found second from the top of Maslow's pyramid. At the top of the pyramid can be found what is often referred to as self-actualization. In our Christian terminology we would refer to that as finding our true place "in Christ," and becoming all God created us to be. Truly, we are all seeking something. In John 1:38 Jesus turned to two soon-to-be disciples (Andrew and John) and said, *"What are you seeking?"* If ever a question demanded an answer, it's that question.

Yes, we are all seekers. But have we set priorities, have we stopped to evaluate the true worth of what we seek, will it bring real joy, will it lead to a balanced life, will it honor God?

Much that we spend our time seeking remains ever so elusive. Yet we are told in the Bible that God is available, He is available to all who seek Him. In Deuteronomy 4:29 we are told, *"But if from there you seek the Lord your God, you will find Him if you look for Him with all your heart and all your soul."* Some think that God is engaged in a game of hide and seek and that he somehow delights in seeing us grope in our attempts to find him. Nothing could be further from the truth. Proverbs 8:17 makes a simple statement, *"...those who seek me, find me."* Surely, we must conclude that this straightforward admonition from Jesus in his sermon is a call for the believer to allow the things of God to have chief place in their lives. Jesus has not implied that we are to neglect all other interests in life, nor has He said that it is wrong to seek other worldly objectives. What He is saying is that we must not allow spiritual matters to be crowded out by temporal interests. We are told to seek the kingdom of God and His righteousness, with the reinforcement that the ensuing result will be that God will add to our lives all else that we might ever need. Jesus has given us the assurance that if we make the Kingdom our principal concern, then we will not find ourselves having lost anything temporally.

Isaiah 55:6 says, *"Seek the Lord while he may be found; call on him while he is near."* What is our reward for seeking the Kingdom? First, we will find his righteousness, for you see the Kingdom of God is righteousness. This righteousness is both imputed and imparted. It is imputed (credited) to our account, and it is imparted (communicated) to our souls. Furthermore, we are rewarded with peace, for if we have the Kingdom as the focal point of our thoughts, we will have little time for worry. God is going to care for all our needs, *"...no good thing will he withhold from them that walk uprightly."* (Psalms 84:11)

Jesus also used part of his sermon (Matthew 6:19-21) to talk about priorities as they relate to our treasures. Few things, if any, in this life can be counted on to last. Quality is an important word to all of us. We demand the best. We want the best automobiles, the best houses, the best clothes, the best investments, the best education, the best of everything! Yet no matter how finely crafted, no matter how expensive the materials, no matter the time dedicated to the making or creating of the object, it will not last. At best, it is temporary. Little wonder then that Jesus made a point to encourage us to have as our treasures those objects that have more eternal value. How sad to invest all of one's life in the building and acquiring of the "best" of this world only to find that it has no lasting, eternal value. Jesus spoke of the futility of seeking to attain that which moth and rust could destroy, and thieves can steal.

Jesus said, *"For where your treasure is, there your heart will be also."* Set your priorities and your heart will follow. Our desire ought to be that we would never lose our heart to this world, for this world is only a staging ground on the way to the only world that will last. If all our interests are here on this earth, then we will have a most difficult time thinking about leaving. However, if our thoughts and priorities are centered in the world beyond, this world will never be a major distraction or attraction for us. We will constantly be evaluating all that we do considering spiritual reality.

How do we go about laying up treasures in heaven? Jesus just meant that we are to do all that we do for the glory of God. It means that we will never put earthly gain above heavenly investments. It means that will not allow materialism to enslave our hearts (dominate our lives), for we have been set free by the Spirit of God. Paul told Timothy that God has given us all things to enjoy, but we must never allow those things to possess us. We must not conclude that Jesus was in any way saying that it is wrong to possess property or gain wealth. There is no virtue or piety found in poverty. It is important to understand however, that if we neglect our spiritual priorities, we are probably dangerously close to covetousness. Who is a covetous person but he who has a case of "mixed up" priorities. We should always remember that money cannot buy the most important things in life: (unknown author)

Money will buy:
A bed, but not sleep;
Books, but not brains;
Food, but not an appetite;
A house, but not a home;
Medicine, but not health;
Luxuries, but not culture;
Amusement, but not happiness;
A crucifix, but not a Savior.

As you begin to evaluate your own personal priorities, remember the admonition of Jesus to lay up treasures in heaven and to seek the Kingdom of Righteousness. If you get this part right, you are now well on your way to financial freedom.

THE PRINCIPLE OF PROMISES

As believers we know the Bible to be a book of promises. Promises that we can depend on in life. Promises that can encourage, strengthen, and expand the faith of the child of God. Promises tested by the ages and found to be true. Promises never to be broken. Promises that come to us in the form of God's Word and are as immutable as God Himself. Promises that are based on the integrity of Jehovah. Politicians, associates, businesses, friends, and even family may often make promises which are soon broken, but God's Word is steadfast and sure. 1 Peter 1:24,25 reminds us, *"...the grass withers and flowers fall but the word of the Lord stands forever."*

Clarifying Concepts

To fully understand the promises of God as they relate to how it is that God supplies for his people, there are two concepts that we need to clarify.

First, we must understand this business of need. Paul said as has been stated, *"My God shall supply all your need..."* John 6:8 has recorded the words of Jesus, *"...for your father knows what you need before you ask him."* God operates where need exists. Miracles occur where need exists. Abundant supply is made available where need exists. Most individuals, given the option, would elect to have a carefree life where there were never any shortages and we could have anything we want, anytime we want. It is the need that causes us to seek God, it is the need that provides the opportunity for Him to work. If the need did not exist, I would likely consider myself self-sufficient and would have little consideration for God in my life. In 2 Corinthians 12:9 Paul makes what appears to be a rather strange statement, *"...therefore I will boast all the more gladly about my weakness..."* Rather strange, don't you think? What was Paul trying to say? This is simply Paul's way of saying that he recognized need for what it is, an opportunity for God to work. Paul concluded that verse by saying, *"...so that Christ power may rest on me."* Paul knew that Christ would turn his weakness into strength, he knew that He would turn his need into supply.

One of the greatest examples of this concept is found in 2 Kings 4:1-7. First, we see a picture of desperation. In this text we find a very poor widow approaching the prophet Elisha and expressing a need. She was so poor and so deep in debt that the creditors were about to come to take her sons as slaves to serve as payment of the debt. She had done all that she knew to do, expended all her energy, spent all her resources. In fact, all she had left was a pot of oil. As she approached Elisha, we see the widow's dependence on someone other than herself.

There are three important principles to be found here. First, note her submission to the authority of the man of God. She took her need to him and put herself under his authority. When a desperate need comes to our lives we need to be under God's authority. When a desperate need comes to our lives we need to be under the authority of God and His word. We also note her admission, for she confessed that all she had was a little pot of oil. Often it is our own pride that prevents God from having the liberty to do a mighty work in our lives. Our admission of need, our admission of want, our admission of our own inability to handle our situation is needed for the power and resources of God to be unleashed in our life. Take note of the fact that her need would not have been met had she not taken action to obey the directions received from Elisha. The lesson is clear! We cannot continue to disobey God, especially in matters related to managing money, and expect Him to bless. Having obeyed, we see her deliverance. Once she had gathered the empty vessels and shut the door, she took the little pot of oil that she had and began to pour it into the borrowed vessels. The little pot filled one vessel, then another, then another. On and on it went, filling the borrowed vessels. When the last borrowed vessel was filled, the oil stopped flowing.

That widow had a need, and God met that need in an abundant manner. We are all needy people. We are like sheep in need of a shepherd. We need grace and mercy, we need salvation, we need security, we need to be sustained, we need help in time of crisis, we need direction for our lives. Whatever the need, the source is the same, for God in Christ Jesus can meet that need.

A second concept that needs to be clarified is the matter of prosperity. We have always, it seems, had that crowd who would have us to believe that the application of a few simple concepts is enough to make us all rich. Please understand that this book is not a "name and claim" book. True prosperity is defined by more than the balance in one's checking account or investment account. One might own vast amounts of real estate, have a large investment portfolio, a six-figure income, and still not experience real prosperity. While these statements are true, the Bible does not exclude material riches from its definition of prosperity. Proverbs 22:4 makes a simple statement, *"Humility and the fear of the Lord bring wealth and honor and life."* Wealth comes from God. Scripture is clear that God would have his people prosper:

"Then the Lord your God will make you most prosperous in all the work of your hands...the Lord will delight in you and make you prosperous..." Deuteronomy 30:9

"Honor the Lord with your wealth, with the firstfruits of all your crops; then your barns will be filled to overflowing, your vats will brim over with new wine." Proverbs 3:9-10

With these promises, which clearly seem to indicate that prosperity to some degree was intended for all, one must then ask, "what happened?" From a Biblical point of view, it appears that shortages are often the result of sin, neglect, and the abuse of God's system of economy. Proverbs 6:11 says, *"And poverty will come on you like a bandit and scarcity like an armed man."*

What would cause such an alarming change in fortune to occur? The Bible offers this commentary:

One man gives freely, yet gains even more, another withholds unduly, but comes to poverty." Proverbs 11:24

"He who loves pleasure will become poor, whoever loves wine and oil will never be rich." Proverbs 21:17

"He who works his land will have abundant food, but the one who chases fantasies will have his fill of poverty." Proverbs 28:19 NIV

A stingy heart, an unwillingness to work, a worldly attitude, resources spent on stimulants and associating with the wrong people would all seem to contribute to a loss of the wealth of resources that God intended for us to have. Perhaps the single greatest cause of our lack/want is the fact that we have violated again and again God's principle of management, or stewardship. This will be covered more fully in another chapter.

We then conclude that God is more than able to meet us at the point of our greatest need. His intent is that we have our needs met in a prosperous, abundant fashion.

<u>Sovereign Source</u>

It has been noted that Paul, in the Philippians 4:19 passage, knew that it was the Lord alone who had the ability to meet his every need. God was, is and ever will be the source of all our supply. However, one must ask the question as to how it is that God goes about supplying these needs.

For the ancient Jews during their wandering in the wilderness it was a matter of going out each morning and finding manna on the ground. They would get on their knees, gather manna for that one day (except for the day preceding the Sabbath when they gathered enough for two days), and eat, knowing that God had supplied for their need. It is not likely that many of us have found manna on the ground lately. Yet, God has used other means and methods to supply our needs. Mind you, we recognize that God can elect any method to accomplish his purposes. It does seem that Luke 6:38 gives us a clear picture of the method most often used in this day. *"Give, and it will be given to you. A good measure, pressed down, shaken together, and running over will be poured into your lap. For with the measure you use, it will be measure to you."* The New King James translation adds that this this will be done by men. In other words, God is not just going to give us a thimble full of what we need, nor is he going to give us a bucket full of what we need, but rather he is going to provide a barrel full of what we need. That barrel is going to be brimming over, pressed in and overflowing. Now comes the next question, how does it get in the barrel? You say, well God put it there, and of course He did. This passage, however, is telling us that God uses other individuals to fill those barrels. Have you ever seen a person that just seemed to give and give and the more they gave, the more it seemed they got? That is the principle in this passage. Some believers are living in want and need because they have cut off the flow of God. They began to hoard and then the devourer came, the flow stopped, and they are still trying to figure out what happened. Yes, God is the source, and He wants to use us to keep the barrel overflowing. Do you want a barrel rather than a thimble? Then obey this text!

The perfect illustration of how God works is found in John 6:1-14 in an experience of Jesus. This is the familiar passage known as the feeding of the five thousand. Mealtime arrived as a large crowd had gathered to hear Jesus teach. Ever sensitive to human need, Jesus instructed the disciples to see what was available to feed the multitude. Upon returning to Jesus the disciples informed him that all they could find was a little boy's lunch consisting of five loaves of bread and two small fish, hardly enough for such a large gathering. Considering such overwhelming need and seemingly such limited resources, we hear the language of unbelief expressed by Phillip (for us all) when he stated that the money of the disciples would not be sufficient to buy even one bite of bread for all those present. Indeed! Had Phillip forgotten that the Source Himself was present. By the time Jesus took the small lunch of the little boy and multiplied it as only God can do, we are told they had twelve baskets of food remaining. We have a source that is not limited by what the eye can see, or human logic can reason. Paul said, *"MY GOD"* shall supply...! Yes, we have a source bigger than the bank or Wall Street and He is able.

<u>Spiritual Sowing</u>

Before we graduate from this Biblical bootcamp and move on to another subject there is one final principle that we must mention. This principle of spiritual sowing is found in 2 Corinthians 9:6-11.

The passage begins with a law. Some refer to this as the law of the harvest. Paul's declaration is simply that no person has ever lost anything because they gave to God. It is here that we learn that giving is like sowing seed. The farmer who goes into his field and scatters seed in a limited, sparing fashion cannot expect to reap a bountiful harvest. This law is true in all of life. The more love we give, the more love we receive in return. The more money we invest the larger the return. We will always reap in measure to what we sow. Perhaps it has always been so, but it is certainly true in this day, many people want something for nothing. That is why state lotteries have become such big business. They play on the greed of individuals who want something for nothing, but all of this violates this law, this principle of God, and it will not work. I just recently read about a couple who won, at the time, the largest lottery winnings in the history of Scotland's Euromillions Jackpot. Colin Weir won $257.6 million in 2011. By the time he died in 2019 he had blown through his wealth. He housed his fleet of luxury and antique cars in the castle he purchased for his home. Along the way he bought a professional soccer team, financially supported a now failed political agenda in Scotland and bought as his second home an elaborate mansion. A financial advisor stated that he was spending $131,900.00 per week on his lavish lifestyle. By the time he died most of his one-time wealth was gone. According to a November 2022 Readers Digest report many former lottery winners sum up life after winning with "easy come, easy go." About 70 percent of lotto winners lose or spend all the winnings in five years or less. I have had the occasion to offer financial planning and investment advice to a couple of lottery winners. My experience suggests that the Readers Digest report might be too generous in its estimate that the money is lost or spent in five years. It didn't take that long! Legal and financial advice is worthless if no heed is given to the advice. Another interesting fact in the report is that most winners keep playing the lottery, thinking they will win again. What drives these behaviors? On some level it's the belief that we deserve something for nothing. Readers Digest reported on one family who won big in the lottery and immediately moved into an exclusive neighborhood. They planned a big 4th of July party and invited all their neighbors. How'd it go? "None of them came – they thought we didn't earn our money." Money changes things, and not always for the better. By the way, although I have been told by many lottery playing, church going people, "when I win, I'm going to tithe on the winnings." I'm still waiting on that first check to arrive at church.

In 2 Corinthians 9:7 the Bible calls for laughter in giving. We are told in this text, *"God loves a cheerful giver."* This deals with the motive of our giving. Deuteronomy 15:7-11 deals with giving to help the poor and addresses the issue of doing so with the right motive by saying, *"Give generously to Him and do so without a grudging heart, then because of this the Lord your God will bless you in all your work in everything you put your hand to."* All the giving in the world that we might ever do can be easily discounted if given with wrong motives. Giving out of a sense of duty, or giving just to meet a specific need, or giving only what we think we can afford is not joyful giving. This passage truly calls us to become hilarious givers. When was the last time you heard laughter break out when the offering was taken in church? Remember, God owns it all, therefore He is not short on resources and in need of our money. However, we sure need to give in order to receive the blessings, and we need to do so with a hilarious heart.

Finally in this passage we have the lesson of generosity. In verse eight Paul said, "*God is able...*" Able to do what, is our question? The answer is in verse ten and eleven. God "*...will also supply and increase your store of seed and will increase the harvest of your righteousness. You will be made rich in every way so that you can be generous on every occasion...*" God is liberal in blessing us so that we in turn may be liberal in the way that we share with others and bless them. Paul went on to explain in verse twelve that this type of giving is a "service" to God. This introduces the idea that our giving is a form of priestly service to God. Our giving to God is as though we took a sacrifice into the temple and made an offering to God. Perhaps the most important reason for our giving is found in verse thirteen as Paul tells us that our "service" will cause others to praise God. So, we are to give with a cheerful and generous spirit so that needs are met through us, God in turn then can give to us, and the Lord is praised through it all. This is God's way of keeping His resources in circulation. Our nation works to control the amount of money in circulation. James Garfield said, "He who controls the money supply of a nation controls the nation." Gosh, was he right! The money supply is the total amount of money in the economy at any given time. The government monitors this supply because of its impact on economic activity and on price levels. It can change financial policies that influence the money supply. At the time of this writing the Federal Reserve is aggressively raising interest rates – supposedly to slow down the economy by making money harder to borrow. This is known as contractionary policy. The opposite position is known as expansionary policy – lowering rates, cutting taxes (when does that happen?) and raising government spending (when is that not happening?). If this sounds a bit confusing, it can be. At the present it appears the Federal Reserve and the Federal Government are both confused – at least they appear to be compounding a problem rather than helping solve a problem. We currently have very high inflation – prices are exploding on houses, automobiles, food and most all necessities. To that end, the Federal Reserve has repeatedly raised interest rates. But, at the same time the Federal Government has gone on a spending binge. Contrary policy, right? Well, know this, God has an economic plan too. God's economic plan is inclusive, not exclusive – it works for all ages, all races, all cultures, all incomes and in good times and bad times. God's economic plan is knowable and workable – it is the will of God (his plan for us) and it is presented to us in the Word of God (his written plan). God's economic plan is recession proof and depression proof – everything already belongs to Him and falls under His control. God's economy is about money and wealth and productivity, along with generosity...but, it is also about eternity, past, present and future.

The Bible has much to say about money, and while these thoughts have only scratched the surface, perhaps they will cause you to search the Bible for yourself as you seek His guidance in your quest for financial freedom. One thing is certain, none of us will ever attain that freedom if we ignore or neglect or violate His principles regarding money. May the Bible become your chief source book in matters related to managing your resources. Jesus said, *"you shall know the truth and the truth will make you free."* As you explore the Word and discover the financial truths of the Bible you will find a new sense of security and financial freedom.

CHAPTER 8

The Process: Financial Planning Concepts

So now you have some idea about what financial planning is all about, and you have learned that there are certain roadblocks that have to be overcome. You have also discovered that the Bible is filled with many specific instructions as to how we are to manage our resources while maintaining a proper attitude about money. You are also convinced that God can supply all our needs. Now you are ready to get going, you are ready to get your financial plan working. You are determined to set your financial house in order, but how do you get started? That is certainly the $64,000 question. (For those of you not old enough to remember that was an old game show from more years ago than I care to remember.) So, what does one do to get started, what comes first? This first and most basic step in personal financial planning consist of four important areas (and a few subsets), each of which are covered in this chapter.

CASH FLOW & CASH RESERVES

To budget or not to budget.....in all three of my lives (minister, counselor, financial planner) I have had individuals in for an interview who seemed to be extremely concerned about the fact that there just always seemed to be more and more month left at the end of each check.

I have seen those with dual incomes as well as single incomes express dismay over the fact that they just don't ever seem to have enough, they just can't get by. They seem to work and spend and work and spend but never seem to get ahead. "What's wrong?" they always ask. I always answer with a question, "May I see a copy of your spending plan?" "Our what?" they invariably reply. "Your budget, may I see a copy of your budget?" Fewer than five percent of those I counsel can produce a written spending plan. No wonder spouses argue about money more than any subject, no wonder we have become a nation of debtors, no wonder we are living beyond our means, no wonder our families are in trouble. A budget allows us the opportunity in advance to make choices and to set priorities. One should no more expect to operate a fiscally sound home without a budget than a large thriving business can operate without a budget. Only chaos and confusion can reign where no budget is to be found.

The typical reaction when I bring up budgeting is, "Oh, no, here we go, he's going to cut up our credit cards and take control of the checkbook." What whose persons are really saying is that they don't want to go on living from payday to payday, but they are not ready to alter their lifestyle. However, without a budget we are much more likely to engage in careless and often needless or impulse spending. Truthfully, a budget is very liberating, for it frees one from worry and brings with it a sense of control over a situation that seemed so out of control. In time, a budget will actually give one more money, not less money, and the money will be used to meet your personal objectives. Furthermore, you are very likely "wasting" more than a few dollars each month because of your lack of a budget.

In 1991 we set about to build an office building for our business. We of course secured the property on which to locate the building and secured the services of a contractor. Even though we provided him with a few sketches of what we wanted to include in the building, the first thing he did was to have a set of blueprints drawn. Those blueprints gave him the guidelines for constructing our building. A budget is the most basic blueprint, and one that we cannot ignore if we are to "get a grip" on our finances. Someone once said that a budget was nothing more than a way of showing him how he could not live on what he made. Well, that is certainly not the intent, but rather to show us how we can live (for God's glory) on what we do make. A budget is simply planning what we will spend, what we will save and invest, and what we will give. A long time ago someone told me that a good strategy for planning spending and saving is the 80/20 rule. Spend 80% and save 20%. Not a bad rule, but as Christians we can be a little more reflective and precise. How about the 70/20/10 plan? Spend 70%, save 20% and give 10%. This is a much better plan for anyone, Christian or non-Christian. A sense of generosity belongs in the soul of every person.

Well, let's get started! In the Appendix you will find several worksheets designed to help you get started. Begin by turning to this page titled CASH FLOW – CURRENT INCOME SOURCES. Here you can record all sources of current income, both as an annual and monthly amount. Don't forget to count income that you might earn from investments and Certificates of Deposit. You should count it as income even if you reinvest the earnings. It is still income available to you. If you are already retired make certain you count any pension, retirement plans, Required Minimum Distributions, etc., as well as Social Security. Now turn to the page titled CASH FLOW – EXPENSES WORKSHEET. This page will enable you to take a good hard look at the spending that is currently taking place. A good way to make certain you don't miss anything is to go back through your checkbook for the past three months. Check your register against the worksheet to ensure you have included all your expenses. Watch for items like gifts and personal care. Make certain you include Christmas, birthdays, and anniversaries under gifts. Haircuts, dry cleaning, etc., are included as personal care items. It is important to be all inclusive here. This page doubles as your budget. If you find that you are spending more than your income, then it is obviously time to take out the pencil and call a family meeting and decide how you might better plan your spending. After you have listed your current expenses, you can then begin at the top and ask yourself questions like, "Is this helping me reach my objectives?" "Is this a priority item?" "Is this in God's will for me?" "Are there some things we need to give up?" This is a time for serious assessment and within marriage, input is needed from each spouse. If you are single, it may be a good idea to confide in a trusted friend. Usually, the input of another is of great value in helping us be more honest with ourselves. Obviously, there are counselors and financial planners who can assist in these stages of planning. The important thing now is to get started in this area of planning a budget. The Lord spoke to Moses in Exodus 14:15 and said, "...*why are you crying out to me? Tell the Israelites to move on.*" God was saying it's time to stop praying and get moving. Friend, you already know it's God's will for you to be a good manager of all that is entrusted to you, there is no need to pray about that! It's time to go to work, so get out that pencil and worksheet and get busy.

NO SUBSTITUTE FOR CASH...Cash is King! We have all probably heard that at some point. What I really want to address in this section is what I consider to be the second phase of basic financial planning, equally important with budget planning. What I am talking about is creating and maintaining a cash reserve that can be used for emergencies and opportunities that might arise. The proliferation in the use of plastic money in our society has led many to disregard the need for an accessible source of cash. Some think that when pressed for money all one needs to do is use the plastic to get out of the bind. Such thinking is the beginning of the end. Another chapter has addressed in detail the matter of credit and debt, but here we must reiterate and understand that plastic is no substitute for cash reserves. Where do you turn if you have an unexpected medical bill? What do you do if you are faced with a major automobile repair? What happens if the furnace breaks, or the hot water heater draws its last breath? Without a cash reserve anyone will be hard pressed to meet these extra demands without resorting to less than desirable means.

Before you set financial goals and objectives you must set aside an amount of money that you will keep your hands off until a real emergency arises. I can tell you there is no better way to build that emergency fund than to do so on a regular, systematic basis each month, putting away a few dollars, just out of reach. Your emergency dollars should be saved in a manner so that they are liquid. Liquidity means that it is readily available without any fees or cost to access the cash. This could be in a regular savings account, a money market account, or a money market mutual fund. You are no doubt thinking, "But those type accounts don't pay much in return." You are right, but don't miss the point. These are not investment dollars; these are emergency dollars. You want the money available without fees and penalties and you don't want the value to fluctuate. As a rule of thumb, you should plan to keep about three to six months' income in a cash position. At the very least about three to six months of cash equal to your monthly spending budget. You may need more if you know major changes are pending. Be tough on yourself and create some rules about what will constitute an emergency and cause you to dip into the account. Make certain that your emergency fund remains segregated from other monies. If you have determined that your present cash reserve is not adequate, then determine now how much is needed and how much you can set aside regularly to reach that amount through systematic savings. It is at this point that you must begin to adopt the rule PAY YOURSELF FIRST. Once you develop the savings habit and reach your cash reserve objective you can divert those regular savings dollars toward other financial goals that you might establish.

ADEQUATE PROTECTION

No financial plan is going to be complete without making certain you have adequate insurance protection. Without insurance you put at risk everything that you have worked to achieve. There are numerous serious events which can have a devastating impact on our financial lives. In most of these cases it makes financial sense to use insurance to cover the risk of loss that can accompany fire, automobile accidents, disability, death, theft, illness, and injury. We transfer all or part of these risks to an insurance company in exchange for the payment of a premium. While this section is not intended to be an exhaustive text on insurance, we will at least mention the most common areas of our lives that often require some form of insurance protection.

HEALTH INSURANCE - The issues and the debate within the health insurance industry has reached a tipping point. Both private insurers and the agencies within the public sector that provide health coverage are squeezed by rising healthcare costs and an aging population.Combine that with an increase in the number of uninsured, and like the pressure building in a boiler, something has to give. The Affordable Care Act of 2010 changed the entire landscape of medical coverage. It certainly addressed some key issues that had come to dominate the health insurance coverage conversations. Perhaps the biggest issue was the question of eligibility for coverage. The ACA does open the door for more individuals to find coverage. While I may not agree with most Federal subsidies to pay for such coverage, I certainly know that we had reached a place of critical concern. For small businesses and self-employed persons, good coverage at a affordable cost is still twisting in the wind. Many employees depend on their employers to provide them with the opportunity to have some form of health insurance. Most health insurance will have some form of deductible and stop-loss included in the policy or certificate. There are also certain exclusions that may exist in certain policies. Where no employer sponsored plan exists, or in small family type businesses, the decision regarding health insurance can be among the most difficult and expensive decisions to be made.

Most major medical policies have deductibles ranging from $100.00 to $1,000.00 which must be satisfied before any insurance coverage begins. Following the payment of the deductible, payment of medical expenses is typically made on an 80 to 100 percent basis up to some amount of money (stop-loss). Beyond the stop-loss the plan usually pays 100 percent up to the limit of the policy. Good plans will pay for regular hospital expenses, doctors' visits as an inpatient or outpatient, surgery, intensive care expenses, and prescription drugs. Most policies state what is and is not covered and tend to limit the amount paid to what is considered "usual," "customary," and "reasonable" charges for services.

Other forms of health insurance include HMO'S, PPO's, Long Term Care (Nursing Home), and Medicare supplements which pay some amount in addition to Medicare for those age sixty-five and older. Some politicians of a certain persuasion use Medicare as a talking point in their desire to see the U.S. move to a national system of health insurance (like Canada or France, etc). No one has yet to convince me that that is a good idea. I have typically been a proponent of less government, not more government. Politicians of another persuasion will discuss Medicare and use the term entitlement in reference to the program. If politicians are implying it's an entitlement because those folks "paid" for it and are therefore entitled to it, good. On the other hand, if they are implying that it is a welfare program, I stand ready to debate that individual.

No matter our age, no amount of financial planning is complete – especially retirement planning – without counting the ever-increasing cost of medical care. In the chapter related to retirement planning I have expanded content on Medicare and Long Term Care planning.

DISABILITY INSURANCE – I have often said that this is the most neglected area of financial planning. A disability plan is designed to provide an income to the insured in the event they are unable to work due to illness or injury. The purpose, of course, is to cover the loss of income and thus prevent what could be a major financial catastrophe if the individual was unable to return to work for an extended period.

No amount of financial planning will be complete without an evaluation of the risk associated with disability. It has been said that planning to live is as important as planning to die, and the risk is greater. At age 30 the risk of disability is 3.4 times greater than the risk of death. At age 40 the risk of disability is 3.2 times greater than the risk of death. At age 50 the risk of disability is 2.4 times greater than the risk of dying. Without proper planning the loss of income and an increase in expenses associated with disability can quickly exhaust a family's savings. For those who can qualify there will be some very limited Social Security benefits. We are told that only about twenty-six percent of those who apply for Social Security disability benefits receive any benefits. A lasting disability can lead one to have to sell personal property, create more debt, and reduce one's standard of living. All of this has led many to call disability the living death.

There are many variables and options that go into designing a disability plan. The better plans will be able to provide some type of gradual recovery benefits along with what is called "own occupation protection." This means that your benefits would continue to be paid even if you were able to return to work in some occupation other than the one you were performing prior to the disability. A good plan should also provide benefits to age sixty-five. Of course, these variables might not always be available, depending on factors such as age and occupation. The cost of disability plans is based primarily on age, occupation, and various riders that might be added to the policy.

Disability plans are available as individual policies and/or some employers will make disability plans available to their employees. If an individual pays the premium on the plan, the benefits will be paid free of Federal income tax. If the premium is paid by the employer, the benefits will then be subject to Federal income taxes.

HOMEOWNER'S, PERSONAL PROPERTY & AUTO INSURANCE - Most providers offer at least six types of homeowner's coverage. The first four are for free-standing, single-family homes, the other two are for renters, and owners of condominium and co-ops. What is known as Homeowners 3 or HO-3 is the most popular type of coverage. This policy is designed to cover "all risks" unless specifically excluded in the policy. Under this policy personal belongings are also covered but are typically limited to a specific list of named perils. To obtain the most comprehensive coverage you need to ask for Homeowners 5 of HO-5. If this type of plan is not available, then ask if riders can be added to the HO-3 policy that will extend it to a more comprehensive coverage. To skimp on coverage here could be the costliest mistake many will ever make. Losses in this area can be devastating. A Form Four policy provides personal possession coverage for renters while a Form Six policy provides coverage for those in co-ops and condos. A Condominium Association will usually have a master policy on the buildings themselves. An important feature of a homeowner's policy is the "replacement cost endorsement." This prevents the insurer from deducting for depreciation. Make certain that you are aware of any limits in your policy. Guns, jewelry, silverware, furs, and coins are just a few examples of items that usually have specific dollar limits inside the policy.

When it comes to automobile insurance there are two glaring mistakes many make with their coverage. First, some are still clinging to very low deductibles which serves to significantly increase the premiums. The other issue is the matter of the limits of liability in the policy. Coverage that was adequate a decade ago is woefully in need of updating. The typical policy will have provisions for bodily injury liability, property damage, uninsured motorist, collision, comprehensive physical damage, and medical payments. Some states have begun so-called "no fault" programs which mean that your insurance pays for your claims no matter who is at fault and the other party's policy would pay their claims no matter who was at fault. Again, this is an area where skimping can be extremely costly.

An ever increasing in popularity type coverage is what is called an "Umbrella Policy." This is really a personal excess liability policy designed to pick up where the liability limits of your homeowners and auto insurance leaves off. It will pay up to an amount stated in the policy, usually one or two million dollars, though higher limits are available.

LIFE INSURANCE - To many people, the only thing worse than talking about life insurance is talking about income taxes. I have met young and old alike, rich and those of very modest means, all of whom have some aversion to the subject. We need to think of the death benefits of life insurance as being discounted dollars. This is true because we exchange a relatively small premium for the full-face amount of policy. Few things into which we put our money affords us the kind of leverage we find in life insurance. The basic questions to be answered in the area of life insurance are always how much is needed, what type is best and where does one find it? One thing is for certain, without it a family will have a difficult time maintaining their standard of living if a death occurs before true financial independence has been attained. With many of today's households being supported by two wage earners it is necessary to assess the need for life insurance coverage on both wage earners.

Many planners indicate that it will take about 75 percent of a family's current after tax income, at the death of a primary wage earner, for the family to continue at its standard of living. This does not include an amount for the payment of debts, or a reserve set aside for education or other financial planning objectives. If income were to drop below the 60 percent level a family would typically have to make major adjustments in their lifestyle. Social Security will provide some payment to a family as a spousal benefit until children reach their late teen years. These payments, however, leave large gaps in what received and what is usually needed.

The most basic type of life insurance is <u>Term Life Insurance.</u> Term provides protection for a limited period. The premiums are usually smaller in our younger years and increase with time and can become prohibitive in later years. Term Insurance builds no cash value.

<u>Permanent insurance</u> on the other hand offers the buildup of tax deferred cash values over the life of the policy. Most policies provide for a level premium which is generally more expensive than term at younger ages but remains level as the individual matures in age. The level premium and the cash value usually means that coverage is available for an unlimited period.

Within the category – permanent life insurance – there are many types of these policies with a variety of underlying interest bearing and investment choices available for accumulating a cash value. The most common term used within this category is Whole Life Insurance, with its name somewhat indicative of the terms of the coverage, your whole life. There are other forms of life insurance that are spin-offs of whole life insurance. The list continues to grow as insurance companies become creative in designing and marketing their policies. Universal Life, Variable Universal, Indexed Whole Life and a variety of other products are but a few examples of so-called permanent life insurance. The purpose of permanent life insurance is to provide coverage for the duration of the insured's lifetime, with no increase in premium. The only requirement is that the premiums are paid in a timely manner.

There will continue to be variations of permanent life insurance, but no matter the twist, most policies will have their origin in these. The one exception might be Single Pay Life, which is a permanent type of policy where the owner pays just one premium over the life of the policy. Clearly, there is absolutely no way to say that there is one type of policy that will always be right for everybody. Our needs are different and our circumstances unique, thus requiring a life insurance plan tailored to our situation.

SETTING GOALS

The final phase of this basic step in personal financial planning is goal setting. We have up to this point arranged a budget, established a cash reserve, and made certain that our insurance plans are adequate. It is now time to do some serious work (done prayerfully) in setting our financial goals and objectives. These goals will become the "yardstick" by which we can measure our progress along the way. This area of financial planning involves setting some priorities on your savings and investment plans.

Goals should be well defined, stated specifically, and written. For what purpose do you intend to save and invest money? Your goals might involve the purchase of a home or automobile, or the education of a child, or a dream vacation or retirement at a specified age with a specified income. Whatever the goals they should meet certain requirements.

Goals should be:

1. Realistic...make the goal achievable so you won't get discouraged at the beginning.

2. Appropriate...make the goal consistent with your family's lifestyle and expectations.

3. Time-specific...set a deadline for achievement in order to add urgency and motivation for action.

4. Measurable...include a target such as a dollar figure or timetable to measure your progress.

5. Challenging...make the goal attractive enough to pursue with some excitement.

For myself, I find it helpful to divide my goals into segments of time. May we never forget that our time is not our own. The Psalmist said, *"My times are in your hands ... deliver me...."* (Psalm 31:15 NKJV) There are at least sixteen words in the Bible that can be translated as time. For me, the two most significant are *Chronos* and *Kairos*. You and I live and operate in the realm of Chronos time. It is easily seen that our word chronology derives from Chronos. Often, we think of time moving in a circular fashion, such as the dial of a clock, moving along between sunrise and sunset. Time as we experience it is basically linear – days, weeks, months, years and decades. God certainly operates in time as we experience it. But we need to pay close attention to the word

Kairos. Kairos represents "special times," "opportune times." Opportune time is experienced as we encounter God in such a manner that we might later, as we reflect on it, describe as having been on "holy ground." Those "God-moments" occur when Chronos and Kairos intersect. I want my life to be filled with those moments, and to that end when I begin to set goals and make plans, I pray to ensure that my plans and His plans intersect. As for using segments of time for goal setting, I prefer to think of having short-term goals, intermediate term goals and long-term goals. My preference is to differentiate using these parameters:

- Short-term goals: six months – three years
- Intermediate goals: four – seven years
- Long-term goals: eight + years

For lack of better terminology, I always thought of this as creating different buckets of money, depending on its purpose and when I expected to need the money. Of course, I also created yet another bucket of money which was readily available for emergencies and opportunities.

In goal setting conversations I have long used the acronym, SMART. For a goal to be worth and workable, it must be a SMART goal. That is, it must be specific – relative to the details of what you hope to attain; it must be measurable – otherwise how can you know if progress is being made? , and how will you know when you get there? What actions will you take, and when, in order to reach the goal? While we want our goals to be a challenge for us, if not realistic we will quickly "throw" in the towel and stop; and finally, it must be time-bound. Remember, in creating your financial plan you will have numerous goals, and with each goal you need to put a completion target date in your plan.

WEALTH ACCUMULATION

Wealth Accumulation, also commonly referred to as Capital Accumulation, is the process of regularly putting money aside into those various buckets, and it leads eventually to the topic of investing our money. Being good stewards will likely mean that we can't keep all our savings in a lockbox or money market account. I think Jesus clarified that in a parable. You can find a refresher in Matthew 25:14-30.

INVESTMENT TOOLS AND TECHNIQUES

You are probably bombarded almost daily with an endless stream of mail and perhaps even telephone calls offering you what someone has chosen to call the greatest deal to come along in years. It just can't miss. Or it just might be one of those that offers you wealth without risk, or better yet the one that offers an out-sized return with little or no risk. I am continually amazed at the absurdity of so much that I see and hear, but that amazement is surpassed by the bewilderment I experience when I see how many people invest money in the deal that "just can't miss." Hopefully this chapter will establish some very basic principles of investing that will assist you in making informed decisions about your long-term savings and investment dollars.

I considered naming this chapter Accumulating Wealth but felt it might not fully convey what I wanted to communicate. However, accumulating money, for the right reasons and in the right manner is exactly what this part of the book is all about. You see, basic in our thinking needs to be the idea that all of us, and I do mean all of us, can and should be saving some amount of money on a regular basis. We need to adopt that "pay yourself first mentality" when it comes to deciding how our money will be spent. We would all like to have significant amounts of discretionary income and large amounts of money to invest. Truthfully, if we are to have any significant resources, unless we inherit a great sum of money, we will have to dedicate ourselves to accumulating the money over time. This method of building wealth is in fact Biblical, for the Bible says in Proverbs 13:11 NIV, "...but he who gathers money little by little makes it grow." The Bible further suggests saving and making investments in Proverbs 21:20 NIV, "*In the house of the wise are stores of choice food and oil, but a foolish man devours all he has.*" It would certainly seem that the Bible encourages us to save and invest for the future rather than consume all that we have on the present.

INVESTMENT FACTORS

There are several factors to be considered when investigating an investment. By carefully weighing these factors against your planning objectives (goals) you are less likely to just be a responder. What do I mean by a responder? I have received numerous calls from clients wanting me to make investment purchases for them based on information that they received from a friend of their cousin who heard about this investment from the nurse in the doctor's office, and after all if the doctor thought it was a good investment, it must be great. Yeah, right! Seriously, certain factors, if considered, will enable us to earn the maximum possible return on our investment, consistent with our objectives and constraints.

Folks at church often approach me with a "can't miss" idea they recently heard about from a friend of a friend whose doctor mentioned at a dinner. Now let's be clear, they are not really asking me for an opinion, they are really wanting a confirmation for a decision they have already made – but now may have a few reservations about – and, now want someone to make them feel better about what they have already decided to do, or have already done. Our church would be filled with multi-millionaires if the 2015 scam of the Iraqi "dinar" had been real. Prosecutors say that victims handed over $24 million to the scammers who promised investors an unbelievable return on investment once the dinar (a highly devalued Iraqi currency) value bounced back against the U.S. dollar. I had a doctor stop me as I walked into church one Sunday and asked me this question, "Are you in?" Not being sure what he meant, I glanced toward to forty-foot ceiling in the church foyer and said, "Well, yes, I just walked in." That's not what he was asking. That very night, he said, the dinar was going to make a big "move," and all investors would be wealthy. On the day I am writing this paragraph the Iraqi dinar has a value of 0.00069 against the U.S. dollar. As far as I know, we have no "new" millionaires in our church. There were also the "can't miss" oil wells in Kentucky, and the Uranium mines in Utah, and don't get me started on the day-traders and the dotcoms. Somehow, we need a plan that does not include the lottery or the next "can't miss" opportunity of a lifetime.

<u>Develop a strategy</u>

Reflecting on the chapter in which we discussed goal setting, we remember the tremendous importance of setting goals and writing them down in some format. With each goal, we then need to take the next step of developing a specific investment strategy for that goal. This means that while we will have a comprehensive financial plan, it will also have individual components addressing our goals, and those goals will have an investment strategy.

<u>Time constraints</u>

The strategy that you develop for a specific goal will need to consider the amount of time involved until you are likely to need to use the money. Those investments suited for an education goal that is fifteen years in the future will not likely be investments suited for the goal of purchasing a house in four or five years. The nature of certain investments is that they need to be held for a longer period while others might be more stable and better suited for the short-term objectives.

<u>Liquidity</u>

People usually want to know how soon they could sell an investment and get their money if they had to do so. The ability to sell that investment is called marketability. Many investments have an available market and can be sold and traded readily while others have a limited market and may be very difficult to sell. Liquidity generally refers to the stability of the price of the investment. To seek the best return there is usually some tradeoff between marketability and liquidity.

<u>Risk</u>

No fluctuation in price, high yield, guarantee of principal, money available when you want it with no penalty, no taxes to pay and at least a twelve percent total return annually. Does that sound like the kind of investment you are looking for these days? Sure, who's not? Yet, my point is that in investment planning there are always tradeoffs, and that is certainly true regarding risk. The risk versus reward principle will always apply. A very low risk investment will sacrifice return whereas a high return investment will sacrifice some security. It is important to understand that a risk-free investment just does not exist. World economics are too complex and change too often to expect an investment environment free of risk. Consider the most recent twenty-four months in our U.S. economy and various financial markets. It has been a roller coaster of breath-taking ups and downs. If that makes you just want to stick all your money in the bank, never forget banks fail. It has happened several times in my career as a financial planner. I was even party to a bank failure. I had a CD in a bank (Washington Mutual) that permanently locked its doors. I experienced the Savings & Loan debacle of the late 80's and certainly the massive bank closings in the 2008-2009 great recession (to some extent exacerbated by banks making faulty loans for real estate). The FDIC ended December 2022 with an aggregate $125.4 billion balance. At the end of the third quarter 2022 bank deposits in the U.S. totally $19.36 trillion. Fail safe, really? Just today (March 10, 2023) the Silicon Valley Bank became the second largest bank collapse in U.S. history. Two days prior the bank announced that it needed to raise an additional $2.25 billion to "shore up" its balance sheet. That created a run on the bank and in a two -day window customers had withdrawn $42 billion. It is being called a "hysteria-induced bank run caused by Venture Capitalist. This banks demise comes on the heels of the recently collapsed Silvergate Bank, which catered primarily to the crypto-currency market. My point is not to frighten anyone, but only to keep us harnessed to reality – little in life, and certainly in the world of economics, comes without risk.

The form of risk that typically comes to the mind of the would-be investor is market risk. This is a risk that arises from the price fluctuations in the securities markets. These markets are driven primarily by supply and demand, but as we have discovered, the market is also subjected to political developments around the world, war or the threat of war, Congressional action, etc. If the market is generally declining, and those declines extend beyond 20%, it is considered a "bear" market, whereas a generally improving market is called a "bull" market.

Financial risk arises when the issuers of any investment develop financial difficulties and therefore the investment may not turn out as originally expected. In the case of a bond issue this could result in a default of either the payment of interest or the principal at the maturity of the bond. In the case of common stock, financial difficulties could mean a suspension of dividends or the loss of the entire investment if the company were to become insolvent.

Investors, in consideration of interest current rates, are giving more attention to <u>interest rate risk</u> than at any point in many years. There is an inverse relationship between existing securities and the general prevailing level of interest rates. If the general level of rates moves upward it would tend to cause the price of existing securities to move downward. It is also true that if the general level of rate moves downward, it would cause the price of existing securities to move upward. Market fluctuation and interest rates are not disconnected.

Individuals with fixed incomes certainly know about <u>purchasing power risk.</u> When prices rise, purchasing power declines. During the most recent years the average rate of inflation has been, by most definitions, tame. The official rate of inflation in the U.S. for 2019 was 1.81%, a decline from the 2.44% of 2018. Suddenly, that is not the case. As I write there are even a few economists who have stated that before the end of 2023 it is possible that we once again experience double digit inflation. In 1980 inflation was officially pegged at 14%. We grow lax in our financial planning by discounting the impact of long-term inflation on our plans. The presence of this risk would seem to dictate the need for some form of investment in a portfolio that would protect one against the loss of purchasing power.

There is no one investment that is "right" when it comes to combating risk. This points again to the need to plan and to develop an overall strategy that will seek optimum return considering one's objectives. There are certain techniques that can be employed to help manage these areas of risk. These are discussed later in this chapter. Certified Financial Planners are held to what is called the "Fiduciary Standard," which means they must always put their client's interest first in all matters. Anyone who offers you investment products is bound by "suitability standards," but don't forget, just because it meets suitability standards does not always mean that it is in your best interests. Risk assessment should lead you to what is both suitable and in your best interest.

<u>Rate of return</u>

Perhaps too obvious to mention is the fact that we invest in order to receive a return on our money. This return can come to us in the form of dividends, capital gains, interest, rental income, capital appreciation, etc. Every investor would want the maximum return possible, but it must not be forgotten that the higher the return, usually, the higher the risk involved.

Taxation

While we do not want to allow our concern for current income taxes to become the tail that wags the dog, neither do we want to ignore the impact taxation can and does make on our investment decisions. Every form of investment will carry with it some form of tax responsibility and liability. While some investments will be taxed presently, others may offer some form of tax deferral or perhaps carry a tax-exempt status. In developing an investment strategy, the impact of current taxes must be considered. In some form, sooner or later, the outcome of your investments will appear on a tax return.

These are all basic factors for the investor to consider. The list is not all inclusive, of course. Other factors may be age, health, family responsibilities, your sources of income, and of course your specific goals. A comprehensive financial plan will consider all the pertinent factors relative to your personal situation.

REDUCING THE RISK

Please do not think that I am about to imply that any investment program can take all the risk out of investing. While that cannot be done, it is possible to employ certain techniques that can minimize some of the risk while having the possible advantage of enhancing your return on investment.

One of the most fundamental techniques is that of diversification. If we had all gotten in on Wal-Mart when it was no more than a regional five and dime store, or Home Depot when it was an upstart building supply company, or IBM when they totally dominated the computer industry, we would all be wealthy. Since most of the population does not possess the wherewithal to pick the next big winner, it makes sense to diversify our investment dollars rather than concentrate them into one or a limited few investment choices. An investment portfolio can be diversified by type of assets, by maturities, by industry, by geographical region, etc. There are many forms of diversification, and they all serve to create a more conservative approach to investing.

Another form of risk minimization is <u>professional management</u>. The average investor has neither the time nor expertise required to manage a successful portfolio. The Bible warns the Christian not to be tossed about with every wind of doctrine. In other words, don't believe everything you hear! The financial press is replete with advice on what to do and not do with your money. Books, magazines, television talk shows are filled with "expert" advice. Nick Murray refers to the financial press as "those great expositors of everything that happened yesterday." All too many individuals are dashing about, following first this advice and then that advice, chasing the current trend. These investors are too close to the situation and are typically buying and selling at precisely the wrong time. How can one avoid getting caught up in that crowd? The answer is simple. Professional management! The use of professional management can help control those knee-jerk reactions to events beyond our control.

A third risk minimization technique is <u>dollar cost averaging.</u> This system somewhat makes volatility your friend. If the basic long-term trend in the market is upward, and it has historically been upward, then dollar cost averaging will work. An erratic or temporarily declining market only heightens the opportunity for the investor who is dollar cost averaging. The strategy provides an investor, who maintains steady nerves, who will systematically purchase shares of an investment, regardless of the rise or decline in price, to have over an extended period of time, a lower average cost in the investment, and thus a greater return. A simple illustration is to invest $100.00 per month in a mutual fund. In some months you will purchase less of the fund, all depending on the price on the date of purchase. The technique works if the investor continues, month after month, regardless of the cost. An example of this strategy is the employee, who paycheck after paycheck, invests in the employer sponsored 401-k plan.

Risk cannot be eliminated, but it can be minimized and to some degree even work to the advantage of the prudent investor. Remember, the greatest risk of all is to do nothing.

Fixed Assets

A fixed income security is an investment that promises the investor a stated amount of income periodically. The most easily understood example of this is the Certificate of Deposit into which the investor might deposit a sum of money for one year, and in today's environment receive about 3.45% interest. Or it might be the bond with a stated rate of 4.00%. A fixed income asset will usually have a stated amount of time associated with the asset (maturity), as well as a stated rate of return. In terms of financial planning balance these type assets are included in order to provide a sense of stability and security to a portfolio. The trade-off is of course the fixed rate itself. This means that there exists a somewhat limited opportunity for growth, which in turn means that this type of asset could be exposed to purchasing power risk. It is possible that because of inflation a fixed income investment would not keep pace with the rising price of goods and services. Fixed assets may also be subject to interest rate risk in periods when rates become somewhat erratic. Fixed income type assets are typically found to be a major component in the portfolio of the individual who wants to draw a regular income from his or her investments. As one seeks diversification and balance in an investment portfolio, bonds will often be included in portfolio design.

It is not our intention to discuss every possible type of fixed income security. This chapter will mention briefly some of the more commonly used securities. Fixed income securities could include preferred stocks, corporate bonds; discounted bonds; municipal bonds; Treasury notes, bills and bonds. One might use CD's and even Savings bonds or I-bonds as a fixed income asset to balance equity positions.

<u>Preferred stock</u>

Preferred stock represents equity capital of a corporation, and the claim of preferred stockholders precedes that of the holders of common stock but follows the claim of bond holders. Dividends on preferred stocks are usually fixed and are required to be paid before dividends on common stock. This type of stock does not have a set maturity date like a bond but can be subject to call.

<u>Corporate bonds</u>

Bonds are promises to pay interest at stated rates and to repay the original investment at the maturity date. The various provisions and technical differences in bonds are too numerous to mention in this context. Bonds carry a credit rating based on the rating of an agency who is in the business of determining the viability of believing in the ability of the corporation to fulfill its promises to investors.

Municipal bonds

The most attractive feature of this bond is the fact that the interest earned is typically free from federal and perhaps state and local income tax. Because the rate of return on municipal bonds is typically lower than the return on a corporate bond, it is important to understand what is called the tax equivalent yield. This simply refers to the fact that depending on an investors tax bracket, less return can in fact be a greater return because of the absence of taxes. This calculation will be discussed more fully in the section which deals with taxation.

Mortgage-backed securities

Mortgage-backed securities have gained great popularity with those investors seeking safety and a higher return than they might earn on treasury type securities. These securities are usually pools of home mortgages and are best known as Ginnie Mae's, (short for Government National Mortgage Association) Fannie Mae's (Federal National Mortgage Association), and Freddie Mac's (Federal Home Mortgage Association). Their very name tells us that these investments are directly linked to the financial side of the housing industry. During the 2008 real estate "crash" or bursting "bubble," these securities were not without their problems. Some unscrupulous mortgage bankers and bond rating agencies falsified the quality of the actual mortgages that were "wrapped" within the investment offerings presented to the buying public. Beyond quality, such issues as the required minimum size investment, some possible uncertainty about the amount of money received each month by the investor, and the eventual repayment of principal should be studied and understood by any interested investor.

Bond mutual funds

A bond mutual fund is a professionally managed pool of either corporate or municipal bonds. The fund is usually well diversified and has the added benefit of reinvesting dividends for those who may not wish to receive all their earnings each month.

Zero Coupon Bonds

Zero coupon bonds – also known as an accrual bond - are nothing more than bonds without a coupon (interest payment). In other words, the investor receives no periodic interest payments. However, the bonds are bought at deep discounts from their par (face value). You can invest an amount today and reasonably expect it will grow to the specified amount (face value) at maturity. Even though the zero-coupon bond does not produce current income, be aware that under current tax laws the investor could be required to claim the so-called phantom interest as earnings.

Fixed Rate Annuities

Annuities are investment vehicles issued and backed by life insurance companies. Most will offer the investor a stated rate of interest for a specified amount of time and will then provide a renewal interest rate at specified intervals. An added benefit of annuities is the fact that interest which remains in the annuity will grow on a tax deferred basis.

While this is by no means an exhaustive examination of fixed income assets, it will provide an overview of some of the more common investments. Again, there is no such thing as an investment that is right for everybody. The financial planning process can assist in developing a strategy that can lead to making wise investment decisions based on personal objectives.

EQUITY ASSETS

Whereas fixed assets typically represent debt (you have in effect loaned your money to the issuer and in return receive interest), equity assets represent ownership. While equity assets take many forms, it is the stock market that most individuals associate with this type of investment. Publications abound, claiming to know the right moves to make to always make money in the stock market. The truth is that if anyone knew what the stock market would do for even one day, they would be extremely wealthy. As you engage in financial planning and begin to make investment decisions you should be aware that from a historical perspective the stock market has produced higher returns than almost any other form of investment. While historical results cannot guarantee what will happen tomorrow, they do suggest that some portion of an individual's money should be in stocks or some form of equity investments.

We have already mentioned the risk that can be associated with the stock market. Goodness, following the 'Great Recession" (2008), and beginning in 2014 and extending through 2021 the average stock market return was 14.8%. Beginning in 2014 and extending to the last day of 2022 the S&P 500 has ended the calendar year with a loss for the year only three times. Know that I say this "tongue in cheek," but I officially retired from my financial planning practice in 2019 – and can still tell my clients that I helped them have a great year in my final year - the S&P 500 finished that year with a gain of 28.88%. Since politicians take credit for lots of good things that happen (and never the bad), I am more than glad to take some credit for that great year. You and I both know that there's little truth to that, but it's fun to pretend. Beginning in 1929 and carrying over to 1942 the stock market declined in nine of the thirteen years, and it was our entry into the war that brought a rebound to the stock market. Yet, if you could have invested $100.00 in 1930, and assuming we had invested all dividends, your investment would have grown to about $515,212.00. That represents an average of 9.65% annual return – and think of all the world events since 1930 that impacted the markets. I am not trying to convince you that any certain stock belongs in your investment strategy, but I am saying that equities – which is inclusive of the stock markets – is important, especially to the long-term growth of our money. Don't forget that within this conversation belongs the differentiation between U.S. and Global economies, as well as the vast difference in shares of the so-called "Blue Chips" companies and the small companies. Your professional advisor can help you analyze and evaluate what will best work for you. Types of equites include:

<u>Common stock</u>

Common stock represents residual ownership of a corporation that is entitled to all assets and earnings, after other claims have been paid. This means that the stock is ownership equity. An investment in common stock requires careful research and understanding of some basic principles. It is not the scope of this book to cover the details of those basics, but consideration should be given to price/earnings ratio; earnings per share; debt to equity ratio; return on equity; book value per share; and of course, dividends.

Real estate

An investment in real estate can be something so primary as the residence in which we live, or it might be some form of commercial real estate or even rental properties. The investors involvement in the real estate may be direct, where outright ownership and management is involved, or it might be indirect, such as would occur in a real estate limited partnership or a REIT (Real Estate Investment Trust). As with any investment, there are risks and rewards associated with real estate. As recently as the early eighties many people seemed to think that real estate would never do anything except continue to climb in value. However, some of those same individuals have discovered that real estate, like any investment, is cyclical and that values often rise and fall for reasons that have little to do with the actual value of the property. Goodness, we are currently experiencing a period where the supply and demand for residential real estate has sky-rocketed home prices. However, I also remember the period sometimes referred to as "The 1980's Oil Bust." The city of Houston, TX was devastated. Oil prices collapsed and soon everyone realized that the fallout was reaching into most facets of the economy, especially banking and real estate. Between February 1982 and March 1987 unemployment soared – one out of every eight workers – in Houston was unemployed. People walked into banks and handed over the keys to their house....and walked away. Cheap money was not so cheap after-all. In 1986 oil fell to $10.00 per barrel and banks began failing like the house of cards they had become. During 1988 more than 3,000 home foreclosures took place every month. Remember earlier when I mentioned the old song...."Spinning wheel.... what goes up must come down....?" Again, always diversify.

Hard assets

Some investors find great appeal in tangible assets. Hard assets become more popular when the general economy stagnates or declines. Investments may range from gold and silver to precious stones and may even include oil and gas investments along with other commodities.

Mutual funds

Mutual funds exist in numerous forms, having varied investment objectives, management styles and of course a variety of underlying investments. Mutual funds are formed when individuals pool their resources so that collectively they have tremendous purchasing power. These funds offer a convenient and affordable way for even a modest investor to capitalize on equities in a manner they could never do on their own. The benefits of mutual funds include diversification, professional management, liquidity, and the opportunity to purchase small increments of the particular investment. The aspect of professional management can be especially appealing because it removes the need for a day to day, hands-on involvement for the average investor. Mutual funds have come to play a major role in the financial planning of a vast number of Americans. Professionally managed funds tend to fall into these categories: money market funds, fixed income funds, tax exempt income funds, growth and income funds, growth funds and specialty funds. Of course, there are numerous subsets of those categories.

Each category has its own set of parameters in terms of objectives and risk factors. Mutual funds will fall on the risk scale according to the underlying investment of the fund. Today's mutual fund possibilities are almost endless. There are closed end funds, open end funds, index funds, target date funds (discussed in detail in another chapter). When investing in any mutual fund I use the four P's to do a basic inventory of the fund and its potential suitability for me. First, what is the *purpose* of the fund? In its simplest form, does it focus on growth, growth & income or income. Furthermore, what is the strategy the fund uses to fulfill its purpose. Regulations require that this information be disclosed in an annual statement. Within in the realm of the *portfolio* we want to know something about the companies the mutual fund managers select, and what trading patterns and systems they might utilize. We can also determine the size of the companies the mutual fund primarily uses, such a large cap (cap=the capitalization size), or mid cap, or small cap. The portfolio itself, and the stated purpose of the fund will also be defined by the typical location of the companies represented in the fund, either domestic or international. The third P is the *price* of the fund. One fund, holding the same investments and having the same managers, is likely to be offered in multiple "share classes." Each share class, usually denoted by a letter of the alphabet, has its own pricing structure. That means two individuals owning the same mutual fund, but in two different share classes, will be paying a different price for the same mutual fund. The final P is the *potential* for the fund. In other words, how has it performed relative to the market, but even more so, against its peer group? Remember, the purpose of the fund will have a direct correlation to the potential performance of the mutual fund. And never forget, past performance cannot be considered an indication of future performance, it is simply a tool to measure the fund managers against their true peers.

EXCHANGE TRADED FUNDS (ETF)

Exchange Traded Funds bear resemblance to mutual funds. They are most similar in the fact that they are both managed "buckets" of individual securities (stocks, bonds or other stipulated objectives). Both tend toward broad diversification within their portfolio and are capable to spanning the globe or having a much narrower focus. There are two significant differences in mutual funds and ETF's. First, most ETF's take a passive approach to ongoing management of the portfolio. Many ETF's use an index to determine what belongs in the portfolio. Mutual funds typically have an investment management team actively analyzing securities and deciding what to buy or sell and when to make those decisions. The active versus passive style of management, as one would expect, leads to a pricing difference and ETF costs are typically lower than a mutual fund. Another notable difference is how both are traded. Mutual funds are traded at the end of the day, on any day the markets are open. An ETF trades within the day – just as common shares of any stock is traded. ETF's have become very popular within broker-dealer platforms known as "managed accounts."

VARIABLE ANNUITIES

Variable annuities could be the investment of choice for those looking for growth opportunities coupled with a form of tax relief, and the promise of an income that cannot be outlived. As part of the retirement planning conversation the guarantee of income is an attractive option. This investment typically allows the investor to select from a diversified portfolio of mutual funds which have been positioned within the annuity, and because they are within the annuity, the dollars grow on a tax deferred basis. The better variable annuities offer the investor the ability to make unlimited exchanges among the underlying funds and this is done with no immediate tax consequences. This means that investment gains could be "captured" without seeing profits eroded by taxation. From my perspective annuities get a bad "rap" from some TV talk hosts who are self-proclaimed experts as well as some financial cannibals who spend multi-millions on advertising campaigns telling you that they are the only guys in town who know what's best for the rest of us. Are annuities right for everybody. Gosh no! But the peace of mind of a future guaranteed income might come in handy for some folks.

In our current investment environment, there are many variations on the "what" and "how" one can invest. Some of what, and how, is straightforward. Other components of what and how can be rather sophisticated. From Private Placements to Cryptocurrency, to the most basic mutual fund, the complexity and sophistication of an investment does not in and of itself make it a better investment. So, what is the best investment out there? Whatever the form of investing that is suitable and appropriate for you, and is compatible with your financial planning objectives, and is in your overall best interest, is the best investment for you. While my goals may have some similarities with yours, it is still going to be a unique process for both of us to find those investments that meet our needs. It is important to maintain a long-term outlook. Shortsightedness in the world of investing can be disastrous. It is critical that any investor understand the importance of staying the course. Those who chase the fads or those who out of fear, are constantly looking for the next investment move to make are likely to be those who discover that a trail of losses is their reward for lacking a long-term approach to investing. Investing is the vehicle which leads us to the accomplishment of our goals and objectives and is therefore not an end to itself. However, wise investment decisions will be a chief component on our journey to financial freedom. I suggest you review the section in Chapter six where I discuss the psychology of money.

We will conclude this chapter with a reminder.... The implementation of any financial plan, especially the use of any chosen investment strategy, will require not only sound strategies, but also equal parts discipline.

Financial planning is part design, part direction, part determination, and part discipline. Often it is the discipline component that separates the good from the great. We find that true in sports, in business, in relationships, and certainly in matters related to our own financial and economic successes. We must have the discipline to plan, the discipline to live below our means, the discipline to save rather than spend, and the discipline to prayerfully read, study, and obey our Bibles. I have mentioned this in other parts of this book, but here I am emphasizing the importance of filtering out the daily noise from the financial news, which can create doubt and greatly muddle our ability to make sound decisions. My financial career serves as proof that investors who spend hours watching market reports, reading several daily newspapers and then fretting over what did or did not happen – in some journalist opinion – in the "market." Yes, we need to be educated and knowledgeable, and yes, we need to be conscious of the overall state of the economy, but we should not constantly find ourselves thinking "I need to do something – my financial advisor needs to do something." Yes, if we have something that needs changing, then let's change it. But all too often we mere mortals make some poor decisions when it comes to our money. I can assure you that the notion that we can somehow "time the market" borders on ludicrous. I once had a client, back in 2008 pull out of the market and move into cash, and say, "We'll get back in when the time is right." Well, sure enough the market, as measured by the S&P 500, did continue to move down, until hitting its low mark in March 9, 2009 when the S&P 500 closed at 676 points (on March 6 it fell briefly to 666 points – how do you like that number). Over an 18-month period it had fallen nearly 60%. Now the client has more than $2 million sitting there in cash, waiting for the right time. Obviously, now the question becomes, when is the right time to get back in? July 2009? October 2009? January 2010? January 2015? March 2019? Then 10 years later, in March 2019, we could look back and see that the S&P 500 had delivered a 10-year annualized total return of 17.8 % - per year. So how did the investor fair in that ten-year window. Well, the time never seemed right, therefore the money had remained in cash, earning an unremarkable money market rate of less than one percent.

We should note that the S&P 500 has gone up 72% of the time year over year since 1926, and its upward movements have tended to be significant. The S&P has risen more than 10% or more during 56% of the years since 1926. The S&P has been down 10% or more only 12% of the time. What is my point? Keep a long view, stay focused, refuse to allow short-term knee-jerk reactions to lead you into undisciplined reactionary buying and selling. Stay disciplined. I am not saying that there will not be a particular investment, that from time to time, will need to be sold and removed from your portfolio. I am saying it's a fool's game to think that we, or anyone else, is smart enough to time the stock market. The evidence is overwhelming – the more you trade, the more mistakes you will make. Create a financial plan, commit to the plan and enjoy the fruits of your disciplined approach to financial planning.

CHAPTER 9

The Purchase: Colleges, Cars and Cottages

I deliberately segmented these three specific topics into this chapter titled "The Purchase" because they share something in common – all three are expensive. Not only are they all expensive, but we also tend to create debt relative to these three purchases, and in many cases that debt extends into many years. A book on prudent financial planning surely ought to spend time addressing the challenges and costs associated with funding a college education, buying automobiles and the mortgages usually affixed to the houses we choose to buy. Along with planning for an eventual retirement these three C's will represent some of our largest expenditures.

PLANNING FOR THE COST OF COLLEGE

This section is included to enable parents and grandparents the opportunity to consider the expenses involved in planning a child or grandchild's college education. I have included grandparents because as both a parent and grandparent I was blessed to be able to assist my children and grandchildren with attending and graduating from schools and colleges without any debt, and in the more than three decades of work as a financial planner I found grandparents often helped their grandchildren with some of their college expenses. The average college student loan balance at the end of 2022 was $34,574.00, and the total federal student loan debt balance was $1.63 trillion. The average debt after having attended a private college was $58,600.00. The so-called ideal time within which to pay off college debt is 10 years. However, according to educationdata.org the average borrower takes 20 years to repay the loan. In the first 5 years of making payments only 45% of student borrowers decrease their balance, with 21% seeing their balance increase. Add on graduate school for a master's degree and the balance increases substantially to $58,300.00 and then extend that into doctoral program and the loan balances range from $101,200.00 - $175,600.00. All of those are staggering numbers. The average salary for people with a doctoral degree is about $97,000.00 annually. Goodness! With the move toward a more specialized society there is no escaping the need for college or some type of training or vocational school. To be competitive in the job market there will be no substitute for some type of higher learning experience.

It is at this point that many families, fully aware of the need for college, find that their already strained budgets will be bent to the point of breaking with the added expense of college. While the average rate of inflation has currently been manageable (2022-2023 has seen an exponential rise in the inflation rate), the annual increase in the cost of a college education for several years lingered around 8 percent. Some providers in the tuition financing business, including finaid.org, report that the 8% number is a realistic number to use in calculating future costs for college. Using that 8% rate of inflation, tuition will double every nine years. For parents with young children the cost of a four-year education could well reach six figures by the time that child graduates from college. The good news for those with young children is that time is on their side. By starting early there is indeed time to accumulate a considerable sum of money that can be used to help fund college expenses. College planning, using those projections, can become a daunting task.

There are still financial resources available in the form of grants, scholarships, and loans. Grants and scholarships typically do not have to be repaid, while of course, loans must be repaid. Some educational loans are available at lower-than-average interest rates and often are backed by the federal government. These loans have been extremely popular through the years, and recently have been in the news as a political "hot potato." It is typical that the repayment of a student loan does not begin until nine to twelve months after graduation and can be extended overall several years for repayment. Based on family income and other factors, some forms of grants do exist. The dollars for these programs usually come from the federal government and are awarded based on need. Scholarships are available in a variety of formats, with many based on academic qualifications. There are scholarships that are based on leadership, citizenship, etc. and of course those that are based on special interests. I recently heard a college recruiter say that the annual listed cost of attendance at any college is simply the beginning point of the eventual negotiated cost of attendance. While there could be an element of truth in that statement, current reality says that college costs are rising faster than most incomes are rising, and that puts additional strain on parents and students alike. As a financial planner I usually advise parents to plan to save as much as possible toward college cost, simply because most other forms of funding for educational expenses are beyond our control and therefore may or may not be available. Although I saw it happen repeatedly, I always cautioned parents that it is seldom a good idea to sacrifice retirement savings for college savings. If parents must wait until after college educations are paid for in order to seriously begin funding their own retirement, playing "catch-up" will be extremely difficult. If you must choose, fund your retirement, then look for creative ways to help children manage college expenses.

Relative to college planning there are several thoughts worth our consideration. In my financial planning sessions with clients, I have often encouraged parents to consider local community colleges as an affordable and accessible means of beginning one's educational journey. As a comparison I will use the local community college, Chattanooga State Community College and the four-year university, the University of Tennessee at Chattanooga (UTC). The current semester tuition at Chattanooga State is $2,565.00 versus $9,848.00 at UTC. Those numbers do not include fees, books, room and board nor any out-of-state tuition costs. Some states, including Tennessee, have the Hope Scholarship which can be applied against those numbers. Most of the community colleges offer transfer tracks that guarantee the students that all the course work completed at the local college will transfer to a senior college where the degree program can then be completed. Tennessee also has a program for those who wish to return to college to complete a degree (Tennessee Reconnect). Many states have such programs available.

Another factor that I discuss with clients relates to the percentage amount of the total college expenses they want to plan funding. Some parents will state that they want to be able to fund 100% of the cost and others will say they want to plan to fund about 75%, and some even less. My personal experience was that of primarily working my way through college, and I still managed to graduate in less than five years. I attended both Samford University and the University of Mobile – both small private colleges - to complete my undergraduate degree. Remember, I began college in the late sixties and costs were much, much lower, but so were incomes and other opportunities. I was blessed to have a scholarship that covered one-half of the cost of tuition. However, there was still rent to pay, a car payment and all its other expenses, books, fees and oh yes, I had to eat, and wear clothes and all the other necessities of any other individual. So, I worked. In addition to Chattanooga, I spend a lot of time in Tuscaloosa, Alabama, home of the University of Alabama. I encounter working students throughout both cities, and in my conversations with them, I always commend them for their determination and diligence in their educational pursuits. By the way, when I encounter these students working as servers in a restaurant, I am always very generous with the gratuity. I admire them for their work ethic and determination. Some universities still offer work-study programs that can help offset tuition expenses. And yes, there is the Federal Student Aid program. It all begins with the FAFSA (Free Application for Federal Student Aid). This is a cumbersome and lengthy process – with many deadlines – so I suggest you go on their website and become familiar with the process and the requirements.

While we would all like to think that our children will qualify for scholarships or some type of grant, the truth is that we need to plan to fund through savings and investments as much as possible. Some type of systematic savings program, possibly by using a 529 Plan (a tax advantaged account used to pay education expenses). Anyone who wants to save for a child's education can open such a plan. The funding for a 529 plan often involves the use of a mutual fund. The Coverdell Education Savings Account is another type of education account that has certain tax advantages, including the tax free growth and spending of the money in the account (if all regulations are met). You should explore any state-specific college funding plans that could exist in your state of residence. These plans provide a way to accumulate funds for college, and many of them will also lock in college tuition rates at present days costs. The Uniform Gifts to Minors Act (UGMA) allows the gifting/transfer of money to a minor and can be held inside the trust account and used for the benefit of the minor. At age 21 the beneficiary (child) will become full owner of the account. These are a few of the most used means of setting aside educational funds for children and grandchildren.

The funding of these various plans usually has many savings and investment options available. Your financial advisor will be able to show you the many options that exist.

BUYING OR BUILDING A DREAM HOME

Smart home buying can be, and probably should be, a diligent and deliberate process. Yes, it is about getting a "roof over your head," but in the long term, at some point, buying a house becomes an investment. Like all investments, the process should include planning and deliberation. As I write this section of the book, we are in a wild and crazy phase in the real estate market. Most recently mortgage Interest rates were under 3%, and the prices of houses have been dramatically escalated – rising from the median U.S. price of $258,000 in 2019, to $385,000.00 in January 2023. The year 2022 saw the escalation of prices slowing to the point that the year over year rise (December 2021 versus December 2022) for the month of December was 2.3%. While some predict declining home prices in 2023, others state the shortage of housing inventory will keep prices higher. Real estate is a tangible asset, and like other assets its pricing and valuations fluctuate due to changing events, needs, availability and demand. In 1975 I bought a three-bedroom brick house for $21,000.00 and took out a mortgage with a rate of about 10% to finance the purchase. In 2006 I sold a four-bedroom, 3400 square foot house for $655,000.00. Some gap, huh? I enjoy grabbing the copies of the local real estate sales guides that agents and builders publish each month. I typically find them in a few of the restaurants I frequent, and recently took a copy of the January 2023 guide. The prices were jaw-dropping. Houses that I would have guessed were selling in the $250,000 range were listed as "priced from the low $360's." We all know what that means, right? It means one house at that price and all the others will be priced higher. At the present, as I am doing research for this book, what appears to be on the 2023 -2024 horizon for home buyers relative to prices and mortgage rates is perhaps a slight moderation in recent trends. Clearly, in some parts of the U.S. the real estate markets are already seeing modest pull back in prices and volume of sales. The same is true in the mortgage industry as rates have experienced modest declines.

My experience in finance has been, no matter the asset – stocks, bonds, gold, oil, commodities, etc. – the pattern can aptly be defined by a song titled, "Spinning Wheel," by the group Blood, Sweat & Tears. The first line in the song says, *"What goes up, must come down...."* Watch, and wait. It's called a correction, and if it goes on long enough and deep enough it's called a recession. Keep your eye on the spinning wheel.

Your financial advisor can help you with deepening your understanding of such things as the tax benefits and the after-tax rate of what your mortgage will cost you, and that could help you determine when, from where, and how much you elect to use as a downpayment on your home purchase.

I LOVE CARS!

I am likely the last person on the face of the planet you should seek out for advice on purchasing an automobile. I do know a great deal about how to buy and/or lease a car. I should, because I have owned over sixty cars in my lifetime. I bought my first car when I was fifteen years old. My Dad refused to allow me to buy a motorcycle and told me that when I was old enough to drive, I could buy a car. Well, I did! My children and grandchildren think that if I have owned the same car for more than eighteen months, I must be sick, and they begin to inquire about my health. I know, funny! But it's the truth. I've owned a lot of cars I wish I had held onto; the 1957 Chevy, a 1962 red Corvair convertible, a 1967 Malibu, the red 1984 Alfa Romeo Spyder convertible, a red Mustang convertible, and while I presently have three cars in the garages of my house, all of those just mentioned are long gone. This is the one topic where, as a financial planner, I should say, *"Do as I say, not as I do."* Now, don't misunderstand, I don't regret owning all those cars – well maybe two or three which were terrible lemons – but by now you have figured out, I like cars.

Currently the automobile industry has been impacted by the COVID pandemic and the ensuing shortages and labor issues. Inventories have been minimal, and those needing financing in order to purchase a car are finding auto loan rates have risen significantly. Gasoline prices, along with rising insurance rates, and the rising costs associated with maintaining an automobile, have put added pressures on the buying decision for many people. Chapter four, which addresses the use of personal debt, can serve as helpful information if considering using an auto loan for a car purchase.

There are several online calculators that will assist in determining the wisdom of leasing versus purchasing a vehicle. Business owners may find that leasing a vehicle has some tax advantageous that make leasing a car a viable option. Some buyers are attracted to leases because it allows them to purchase a more expensive vehicle with smaller payments. Just remember, leasing a vehicle is paying rent for the opportunity to drive the car. My friend Brent Morgan is the owner and CEO of Integrity Auto Group. He has a Chevrolet dealership, as well as a Cadillac-Buick-GMC dealership. They recently added a Mazda dealership to their lineup. It is always interesting to discuss the significant changes taking place in the auto industry. His expressed fear around all the current frenzy related to electric cars (EVs) is that China has a massive monopoly in the production of lithium batteries. I can see where this is headed, how about you?

Owning or leasing an automobile will be a significant line-item in your budget. Plan carefully, be realistic, don't be unduly swayed by the sights and sounds of the showroom, separate the process from your emotions. While many of you readers will be too young to remember the TV show "Dragnet," whose primary police detective character was Joe Friday, we all need to adopt his favorite line, *"Just the facts, sir."* It seems the Bible also offers that same advice, *"Get the facts at any price, and hold on to all the good sense you can get."* (Proverbs 23:23 LB) As one who has "shopped" for many cars, I offer one more word of advice. This too comes from a TV show about law enforcement. Each episode always contains a scene when the sergeant is dismissing the officers from roll call, and they turn to walk out the door – the sergeant always says, "Be careful out there."

CHAPTER 10

The Payment: Paying Less to Ceasar

How do you keep more of what you earn? One way is to write a smaller check to the Internal Revenue Service. No matter our distaste for paying taxes, it is a way of life. Most of us realize that the payment of our taxes provides for some of the most basic services (roads, protection, etc.) that we often take for granted. At the same time, none of us should be willing to pay more than our fair share of taxes. Paul said in Romans 13:7, "*...if owe taxes, pay taxes, if revenue, then revenue; if respect, then respect; if honor, then honor.*" Jesus was asked if His followers should pay taxes, His reply is in Luke 20:25, "*Then give to Caesar what is Caesar's, and to God what is God's.*" While I do not have to agree with everything the governmental authorities spend tax money on (in fact I strongly disagree with much that is wasteful and counterproductive), I do have an obligation to pay taxes. However, I do not have an obligation to pay more than I must pay! For that reason, tax planning is an integral part of financial planning.

TAXATION 101

We are all acquainted with the fact that taxes come in an assortment of sizes and shapes. We pay sales taxes, gasoline taxes, real estate taxes, income taxes, death taxes, inheritance taxes, gift taxes, and estate taxes.

This chapter will deal only with income taxes and will give only a broad-brush approach to the subject. One's tax advisor can of course provide detailed information.

One's gross income is the sum of all wages, salaries, business income, interest, dividends and realized profits from investments. Your adjusted gross income is calculated when you subtract certain items such as IRA's, alimony payments, etc. from your gross income. From your adjusted gross income, you may subtract itemized deductions for things like charitable contributions, sales taxes, unreimbursed expenses related to employment, mortgage interest, etc. For those who don't itemize there is a standard deduction. Frankly, these days the standard deductions have risen to the point where it is more advantageous for many tax filers to simply use the standard deduction. If itemizing, you will be using Schedule B and listing those items that are deductible and subtracting them from taxable earnings.

We often talk about tax brackets, or tax rates. What is referred to as the marginal rate is the amount of tax that will be paid on the next dollar earned. The tax bracket will be determined by the last dollar earned. The marginal rate will depend on things such as income, filing status, etc. The effective rate, on the other hand, is the total amount of taxes paid, divided by your adjusted gross income. The way you can keep more of what you get is to reduce the effective rate, thus keeping more dollars at home with you so that you can invest them toward your objectives.

STRATEGIES THAT REALLY WORK

Ask any accountant or tax preparer what their busiest time of the year is, and they will tell you April and December. That may be the time when you prepare your forms and file them, but that is not the time to engage in tax planning. It never fails, every year I receive dozens of calls beginning about mid-March from those individuals who are seeking ways to reduce their income taxes. Frankly, they should have been planning the previous March for the now current year. Under current tax law there are certain strategies that still make available to us the opportunity to minimize our income taxes. Remember, our federal tax regulations are often in flux, and can impact what we can or cannot do to better manage personal income taxes.

DEDUCTIONS

Obviously, those persons who have certain business expenses have the ability (with some limitations) to deduct their expenses. Some of these expenses may be those associated with operating an office, automobile expenses, travel, and entertainment, etc. Even those without business expenses qualify to claim either the standard deduction or to itemize their deductions. The amount of the standard deduction for the tax filing year 2022 is $13,850.00 for those filing single and $27,700.00 for those who are married and filed a joint return. For those of us over age 65 that is an additional $1500.00 exemption if filing as jointly married, or $1850.00 for a single filer. Itemized deductions can include charitable contributions, medical expenses, property taxes, mortgage interest, certain investment expenses, state and local taxes, and income taxes. You will want to make certain that you have not missed any allowable deductions for it represents "found money," money you can use for your own purposes.

DEFERRAL

I want to go into orbit when I hear a client say, "Well I'd rather pay the taxes now, after all, we don't know what the future is going to bring." Anytime I can invest in such a way to postpone paying the income taxes, I want to do just that! Almost any qualified retirement plan will fall into this category. It will also include Individual Retirement Accounts, Keogh Plans / Profit-sharing plans, Money-purchase plans, Qualified defined benefit plans (which are still available, but used less frequently), Simplified Employee Pensions, Tax Deferred Annuities, Tax Sheltered Annuities, Tax Sheltered Custodial Accounts, and Life Insurance cash value. The presumption is that when the time comes to withdraw the cash from these investments one will be in a lower tax bracket and in turn pay less in taxes. Don't forget, IRA's (Individual Retirement Accounts) are alive and well.

DELAY

Some individuals may be in the position to delay the receipt of income each year. Perhaps an employer will be willing to wait until the following year to pay out a bonus or maybe by postponing the sale of an investment or a property the income can be pushed forward into another year. In the case of employers and employees who agree, a more formal deferred compensation arrangement might prove satisfactory.

DIVERT

What do I mean by divert? My reference here is to shifting income to others. The most common examples of this are parents, who are in a higher income tax bracket, and decide to shift taxable income to their children. This can often be done in very simple arrangements known as the Uniform Gift to Minors Account (UGMA) or the Uniform Transfer to Minors Account (UTMA). The UGMA and UTMA are taxed to the child at the child's tax rate (typically zero) if they are over the age of fourteen. The caveat is that the earnings from the trust will be taxed to the child at their parents tax rate until they attain age fourteen. This applies, basically, to earnings that would exceed $1,000.00 per year. The income that is shifted can of course be later used for college expenses, etc.

DENY

Deny paying taxes, how is that possible? The income from some investments, particularly municipal bonds, is free from federal taxation. Any income derived from ownership of the bonds, while reported on the tax return, is not taxed, thus denying the taxing entity the right to collect taxes on income generated from those bonds . For some, with more sophisticated tax planning needs, there are investment vehicles which might create ongoing tax credits, and if considering the sale of highly appreciated real estate, tax strategies exist that can efficiently exchange (1031 Exchange) or transfer (i.e., QPRT – Qualified Personal Residence Trust; and certain gifts and donations) of real estate. Roth IRA's can also be a great – and simple - strategy for creating the potential for future income that will be free from federal income taxes.

GET GOOD ADVICE

The Bible teaches us that wisdom is found by seeking good advisors. Your financial advisor, your attorney and your tax adviser are the right people to guide you in making sound decisions. Just do it! The tax regulations for inheriting IRAs have changed, along with so much of the seldom static tax code. It has become anything but simple. The benefits of good advice are many, including the peace of mind it brings when we seek and heed sound advice.

It is not uncommon to find dollars within a person's tax return, simply because they failed to take advantage of some part of the tax law, or they misapplied the law. For some tax planning starts and stops with trying to get the biggest refund possible from the IRS. Frankly, I spend time planning every year to ensure that I get the smallest refund possible from the IRS. If I get a big return of my money (notice the word "my") then I did a poor job of planning. Tax planning is finding a way to send as little to the IRS as legally and reasonably as possible. I have never received a "thank you" note from the Federal Government (IRS) thanking me for loaning them my money. Furthermore, when was the last time you received an interest payment from the IRS based on the loan you made to them? Seek the help of those professionals who are trained to find every possible means of keeping more of what you earn in the form of income. It is after all, a matter of stewardship. We will never be financially free if we continually pay more than our fair share in income taxes.

CHAPTER 11

The Plan: Has the Gold Tarnished in Your Retirement Plan?

What exactly are the "Golden Years"? Retirement, by definition, is a time when we "withdraw from one's position or occupation." I'm still trying to figure out how that definition is applicable to me. One some level I get it. I no longer pastor a church, but every week I study, pray, prepare Bible studies, conduct funerals, visit the sick, and occasionally conduct a wedding. Pastors do that on a regular basis, but I am "officially" retired from that occupation. But am I?

For thirty-four years I looked forward to going to the office every day and working with clients, assisting them in developing financial plans that allowed them to save, invest and watched most of them turn hopes and dreams into realities. I no longer go to that office. Again, by definition, I am retired from that position. But am I?

Yet, I am writing this book in the hope that it will inspire others to take all the necessary actions to make financial dreams become realities, all while glorifying God. I still conduct seminars and Bible studies and preach sermons that impact the financial and spiritual lives of a lot of people. So, am I retired? Yes, and no, and that's the way I like it. By choice I continue doing so many things that were attached to my dual careers of ministry and financial planning, and I loved it then and now. Then, I did it as a career; now I do it as a choice. And the income dynamic shifted from being paid to work, to doing what I choose to do, not for money, but the joy of doing it. Supposedly, retirement is that time in our lives when we slow down, we spend time traveling and playing with the grandchildren. It used to be thought of as that time in life when our careers would be replaced by hobbies, our vocations replaced by avocations. The thought of the golden years conjured up the idyllic notion of sitting in the porch swing and watching the sun set. In the movies the golden years were preceded by the presentation of a gold watch. Such are our preconceived thoughts of what retirement "should" look like.

Frankly, retirement seldom looks like the scenario described above. On the one hand I have observed a segment of the population who arrive at their appointed time for retirement with a sense of financial independence. For a few that time may come as early as age 50 or 55. Sports cars, boats, RVs, and extensive travel become their newfound toys. However, those are the few! I see a much larger segment of the retired and soon-to-be retired community who are less concerned with their toys but are greatly concerned with how long their retirement income will last. As we retire earlier and live longer this concern will become even more pressing.

THE TIME IS NOW

There are not many individuals who leave their college graduation exercises thinking about retirement planning, but they should! My granddaughter Maggie graduated from the University of Alabama three months ago (December 2022) and is just beginning a career-related job. I have tried to persuade, plead, beg, cajole, and coerce young adults in their twenties and thirties to start planning for retirement. No doubt, many other interests and needs demand attention in those early years of one's working life. There are automobiles and homes to buy, children to educate and a myriad of other demands for our dollars. However, the adage, "the sooner the better," certainly applies to retirement planning.

There is a definite cost to waiting. If an individual would save/invest the equivalent of an IRA - $6500.00 per year – from age 25 to age 65, and assuming an 8% return on their investment (based on past performance, an acceptable assumption for the stock markets), that person would have over $1.683 million. But wait, how many 25-year-olds are doing that? So, they wait until they are 35 years old and set their goal to have over $1.6 million. Using the same return on investment, but with only 30 years to reach their goal, what are their chances of making the goal? Unless they save/invest $14,900.00 per year they have no change of making goal. In my thirty-seven years as a financial planner, I have had several, but not many 35-year-old clients saving that amount of money. Now suddenly he or she wakes up one day and realizes they are 45 years old. What now? You guessed it – more is required to reach that $1.6 million goal. Now with only 20 years remaining to reach goal that individual will need to invest almost $37,000.00 annually. You see where this is going.... Start sooner rather than later! We must make the passing of time and the so-called magic of compounding our ally.

The time to plan for retirement is now. To delay is to jeopardize your financial security when you are ready to enter those golden years. Since most of us can expect to spend 25 percent to 30 percent of our life after retirement, it behooves us to start today. At age twenty-one I began participation in a retirement plan. I "officially" retired 49 years later, and there was never a year I did not contribute toward my eventual retirement. Something that always baffled me, and does even yet, is the federal government's limit on what is permissible to contribute to one's personal retirement savings. Sure, I know why they impose limits....it is so they can collect the taxes on earned income. But, to me, that has just always seemed counterproductive. So, what am I saying? Simply this, save all you can, invest everything allowable and possible into tax advantaged plans, and then find additional ways to prepare for your personal financial wellbeing, in what we all hope are those golden years.

HOW MUCH IS ENOUGH?

While the financial planning process can help you determine an amount that you will need for retirement, most financial planners have long estimated that a person will need between 70 percent and 80 percent of his or her current income as retirement income. Obviously, the amount one will need will be impacted by liabilities, activities, expected travel, and where one lives during retirement. When you begin to calculate a spending plan for retirement, don't forget to account for likely increases in medical expenses, hobbies, travel, and leisure activities. Then of course, you cannot ignore the impact of inflation. Frankly, I consider this thought process and this calculation regarding one's probable income needs in retirement far too important to leave to estimates. This is a time to get it right, even if details bore you, get into the details. Your financial planner will have experience helping you flesh out all the details.

GENERATING AN INCOME

Once you and your financial planner have determined an amount you will need, the next step is to determine how you will generate that income. Perhaps you will have several sources of retirement income. For many decades companies maintained what employees and employers simply referred to as a pension plan. A pension plan is an employee benefit begun and maintained by an employer (or organization) that provides (deferred) income to an employee upon retirement. There are, of course, several types of retirement plans, but the plan long called a "pension plan," is referred to as a defined benefit by ERISA (Employee Benefits Security Administration). You may recognize this terminology from having read chapter ten. ERISA, part of the Department of Labor, administers and enforces all the provisions of the Employee Retirement Security Act. "Defined Benefit Plans" were once the backbone of employer sponsored retirement plans. In recent years many of those plans have been phased out and replaced by what ERISA refers to as a "defined contribution plan." Most employees are familiar with these plans, among the most typical are the 401-k plans, and among non-profits the 403-b plans.

There was a time in our nation's history when company sponsored pension plans where a significant part of a retired person's income. I can remember when I presented what was called the "Three-legged Stool of Retirement Planning." I would sketch a stool with three legs on the board and then, one by one, in succession label the legs as Pension – Social Security – Personal Savings. Defined Benefit Pensions have slowly all but disappeared. Many of those plans reached the point where they were under funded, and many failed. The website for the Pension Benefit Guaranty Corporation states that over 33 million working Americans are participants in an employer-sponsored pension plan. The jeopardy that came to be associated with defined benefit pension plans is affirmed on that website with a link to what is titled the Special Financial Assistance Program, which is PBGC information for financially troubled pension plans. The shift away from defined benefit plans has placed the major responsibility of saving and planning for retirement squarely on the shoulder of the workers. As a financial planner, I was enlisted by a large, national insurance company, to conduct group meetings in which I explained why the pensions were being frozen (no more contributions from the employer) and how employees would need to contribute more to their own 401-k accounts in preparation for retirement. That scenario has repeated itself and is the current reality for many workers. As previously mentioned, the Federal Government places limits on the amount income earners workers can invest in a "retirement" plan (401-k, 403-b, 457-b, traditional IRA, Roth IRA, SEP-IRA, Simple IRA, Simple 401-k and Solo 401-k).

SUPPLEMENTAL SAVINGS

Saving for retirement will fall into two broad categories. First, you might save in a plan that enables you to exclude the amounts you contribute from current taxation. These are known as qualified plans. The other form of savings, called non-qualified, may or may not have certain tax advantages, but the contributions would not be excluded from current taxes.

Qualified plans include plans such as those I listed above. Some of the plans are employer sponsored, while others are directly "owned" by the individual contributor. Generally, these qualified plans will have penalties associated with any withdrawal prior to age 59 1/2. There are excellent options available for the self-employed. Hybrid versions of a 401-k plan and SEP's (Simplified Employee Pension) are staples in the retirement toolbox of sole proprietors and small business owners. No matter the plan, there are limits, and pros/cons of each plan. All the plans provide tax benefits, including the tax-free growth of your money. As previously stated, I will take all the tax deferred growth of my money any time it is available.

Because of limits on the amount wage earners can place into qualified retirement plans, it becomes important, and necessary, to find additional methods of saving for retirement. Non-qualified plans and accounts that are used as retirement planning tools include annuities, deferred compensation plans, executive bonus plans and life insurance cash values. Annuities, fixed and variable, have become a major source of savings for retirement planning. After the deferral stage (accumulation and tax deferred growth), annuities are designed to pay the investor an income they cannot outlive. If an individual elects to receive annuity payments, each payment will consist of part principal and part interest. Only the earnings will be subject to current taxation. Numerous annuity payment options may be chosen for the purpose of receiving the benefits from the annuity. Money placed in a non-qualified plan will have already been taxed on the principal, but it is usually afforded the opportunity to grow in value and have that growth sheltered from current taxation. As we learned earlier, that is simply known as tax-deferred growth of an investment.

In determining our retirement income sources, we must, of course, include Social Security income benefits. Most employees in private industry are covered by social security, as are most self-employed people and members of the armed forces. There are a few exceptions to mandatory participation, including certain religious exemptions, students working for a college while enrolled at the college, aliens working on temporary Visa's, and although it has changed significantly, many workers – who have paid into an already existing government sponsored system – were not required to pay Social Security taxes. Social Security, enacted into law in 1935, can provide disability benefits, survivor benefits, retirement benefits, and medical benefits (Medicare). You are entitled to maximum benefits at age 65 or older, depending on your date of birth. Reduced benefits can be received beginning at age 62. If you were born between 1938 and 1942 you will have to wait until age 65 and 6 months to receive full benefits. Those born between 1943 and 1954 will have to wait to age 66 to receive full benefits. Full benefits will not be available to those born in 1960 until age 67. When to claim benefits is a conversation frequently discussed. Just know this, there is no single answer to that debate. The answer lies within the personal circumstances of everyone. The age-based, so-called, full retirement age benefit was the target for the majority of the clients I worked with through the years. There could be a financial advantage to postpone claiming that income benefit to age 70. I fell into the category of those who became eligible for the "full benefit" at age 66. To postpone claiming that benefit at age 66 and claiming it at age 70 provided an 8% per year (total of 32%) increase in the benefits. However, don't miss the fact that our Social Security benefits are actuarially calculated. What does that mean? Actuarial Science is the science of determining when we are most likely to die. When you buy life insurance the premium you must pay is actuarially calculated. In other words, the insurance company and the Social Security Administration are betting on when you will die. On average they get it right. For Social Security it means the amount of the benefits paid is based on a projection of how long we might live. The SSA is betting that at my current age I will live an additional 12.9 years. If I die sooner, or by that date, they win. If I live longer than that, I win. My point is this – no matter when you opt to begin SSA benefits, actuarially you will receive the same amount of money between your starting age - be it 62 or 70, or a number in between - and a calculated bet by the SSA as to when you will die. The solvency issue with Social Security benefits is not so much that we are living longer, because on average we are not. The issue is that we have fewer workers contributing, combined with the "Baby Boomer" surge of applicants for benefits. Just be wise in determining when you begin your claim for retirement benefits.

WHAT'S UP WITH SOCIAL SECURITY?

In 1935 Franklin D. Roosevelt signed the Social Security Act into law, and the first checks were disbursed in 1940. In its original form workers were required to reach age 65 before claiming benefits. In 1956 the SSA was amended by Congress to allow women to receive benefits at age 62. In 1983 Congress passed a law that gradually raised the "full" retirement age within the Social Security Act. The 1983 amendment raised the age beginning with people born in 1938 or later. Based on an amendment that passed Congress in the 1970's, any person can now apply to begin receiving benefits at age 62. Yet another amendment has made it possible for beneficiaries of SSA to receive an annual cost of living adjust (COLA). Of course, benefits at age 62 are dramatically reduced, and on the other end of the continuum, it has become popular among financial counselors to promote delaying the start of benefits until age 70 in order to gain a larger benefit payment. It is certainly true that we can improve the amount of our benefit by continuing to earn annual credits (based on current income of working) and delaying the start of benefits. In addition to retirement benefits, Social Security funds are also used to payout disability benefits, as well as survivor benefits.

We hear often Social Security is soon to be bankrupt. That conversation has led many Millennials and Gen Xers to believe that Social Security will not be around long enough to provide any benefits to them. But know this, Social Security is not going bankrupt. The Board of Trustees releases an annual report on the financial outlook for the Social Security trust fund, and unfortunately some reporters will take snippets from those reports and use inflammatory headlines about its looming demise to attract readers. I am holding in front of me an article written by an internet-based reporter. His headline reads, "Social Security Benefits Could Drop by 20% by 2032." Yes, there is a smattering of truth in the report, which is framed around a report from the *Congressional Budget Office* (CBO), which indicates that by 2032 -2033 the Old Age and Survivors Insurance (OASI) Trust Fund will be depleted. First, the OASI will not be depleted by 2032 – and if that did happen, those of receiving benefits would still receive slightly more than 75% of our current benefit. The CBO, which tends to have the ear of every politician in Washington, has prepared a list of possible changes that would reportedly stabilize the fund. Thus far, politicians – who make every decision based on the next election cycle – have done little more than talk and point fingers at each other. But do understand this, those "go-broke" dates don't come with full disclosure. Yes, current benefits could substantially drain the Trust, but that does not take into account that Americans will continue to work and continue to make contributions to the Trust. Furthermore, we do need Congress and the CBO to take the issue seriously enough to stop the infighting and develop a sensible plan to stabilize the plan, and to instill confidence in the minds of our American workforce that Social Security does now, and will in the future, be an important component of our retirement planning.

HOUSING AND HEALTH CARE

Special consideration should be given to housing and health care as you begin to plan for retirement. Many plan to relocate upon retirement. Others want to have a second home or a vacation cottage. Still others would like to sell and move into an apartment or condo. The costs of relocating or making additional purchases must be included in the financial plan. Tax implications are also involved if you sell a house and elect not to repurchase. These are significant factors that will have a major impact on one's financial health in retirement. The ideal situation is to ensure that no mortgages are carried over into the retirement years. I have not found anything that brings the level of peace of mind that comes with knowing that no house payments followed me into retirement.

Health care, it seems, is constantly on the mind of those us who are retired or planning to retire. And for good reason! Don't neglect the fact that by age 65 one cannot ignore the Medicare conversation. Even for those who will continue to work beyond age 65 there are a few things that demand our attention. Even if you plan to keep working you still have a 7-month "Initial Enrollment Period" that cannot be ignored. Not complying with the IEP brings late enrollment penalties. Your financial planner can help you navigate the Medicare maze.

Another medical mountain to climb, and one that grows larger by the day, is the matter of long-term care. Presently it is estimated that 17% of the U.S. adult population provides unpaid care to an adult over age 50. Over 75% of these caregivers are women. Many of the caregivers are also employed and raising children of their own. In 2020 that number of caregivers reached 41.8 million people. It is estimated that the monetized value of that "free" caregiving has reached $470 billion of free labor. A bigger wow is that the average length of unpaid caregiving is 4.5 years. An astounding 11% of care recipients require assistance for over 10 years. And, as we know, a large percentage of caregivers – 89% - are related to the care recipient, and they spend an on average of 20 hours per week in active caregiving.

In my book, *Goodnight, Sweetheart,* I trace my wife Judy's battle with Alzheimer's Disease from diagnosis to death. There were sixteen years between those two data points. It was a crushing time for us, and the grief of loss that came with every additional decline in her cognitive abilities – and the ensuing physical disability – was like blow after blow of an unrelenting hammer.... pounding and pounding until the very end. As I describe in that book the emotional cost was incalculable. The dollars and cents ran into the hundreds of thousands of dollars. Had she and I not been wise enough at age fifty to make plans for the unknown, I cannot even fathom what the outcome would have been.

It is estimated that one-third of all those who reach age 65 years will never need long term care. But that means more than sixty percent of us will! And of those, twenty percent will need long-term care for more than five years. The likelihood, and the escalating costs of this level of care, demands that this topic not be put to the side in our retirement plans. Failing to plan for health care, including long-term care can shipwreck all of one's plans. Failing to heed the warnings can bring disaster of Titanic proportions.

You will no doubt think of other concerns related to your own retirement planning. Whatever the concerns, it is imperative that you start planning immediately. A delay can only cost you in money and peace of mind.

CHAPTER 12

The Passage: Where There's a Will, There's a Way

One dictionary defines "pass away" as "to go out of existence." Well, as a Christian I'm tossing that one out the window. The Apostle Paul said, "to die is gain." He also said, "absent from the body, present with the Lord." That doesn't sound like out of existence. To say pass-away certainly sounds less harsh that using the term die. My experience has been the terminology we use for dying is both regional and cultural. This chapter on THE PASSAGE is about dying, but it is more about what comes next. For more details on the spiritual and theological side of that conversation I direct you to my book, *Goodnight, Sweetheart*. This is about our ability to speak from the grave, and in so doing make the lives of those we love easier and better.

One of the first dramas that unfolds in the Bible is the story of Cain and Abel. We remember that Cain made an offering to God that was not acceptable, while his brother Abel made an offering that pleased God. In anger Cain took the life of his brother Abel. In Hebrews chapter eleven, the Bible focuses on the faith of many ancient believers, and it is fitting that Abel is found in that list. Of Abel, Hebrews 11:4 says, "*...he still speaks, even though he is dead.*" This is of course, a reference to the testimony and the faith of Abel. It brings us to an interesting question. Can a person really speak from beyond the grave?

My answer is in the affirmative, for from a financial planning perspective, that is what estate planning encompasses, allowing us the opportunity to have a voice in our financial affairs even after we are dead. We would be totally remiss if we did not mention the tremendous importance of estate planning. There are no doubt many individuals who have gone to great lengths to make numerous plans for their lifetime, but who have done little if anything to plan for their ultimate death and the distribution of their resources following their death. The Bible says in Hebrews 9:27, "...*man is destined to die once.*" Given this fact, it is gross mismanagement of our God-given resources to fail to plan in the matter of our estates. Some would be quick to argue that their estate is too small, too insignificant to warrant estate planning. The most basic issue in estate planning is the simple fact that if you don't provide an estate plan, the State will provide one for you. You may have the best intentions in the world, but unless they are written, they are worthless.

DON'T LEAVE HOME WITHOUT IT

No, I am not talking about your American Express card (a by-line in an old TV commercial). I am talking about your will, that is your LAST WILL & TESTAMENT. Although there are various types of wills, the most common is called a simple will. A simple will usually provide for the payment of debts and expenses; appointment of an executor or executrix; specific bequests; transfer of the entire estate to the surviving spouse, if living; the transfer of property to children and heirs if there is no surviving spouse; and the appointment of a guardian for minor children and their property. This is the most basic of all financial planning tools. Should you neglect this area of planning, the judge and the courts will be delighted to write a plan for you. Your will can be the most important document that you will sign in your lifetime. It is in a real sense an extension of your life and your interests. When should you write a will? Procrastination is probably the chief reason most people do not write wills. Think...the time is now! Remember, a will is not written for the person who has died, it is written for the living. It will make no difference to the deceased if he or she failed to prepare a will, but it will make all the difference in the world to the living. Making a will is spending money, after you die, in ways that you would have done had you lived. It reflects the values of a person, both positive and negative. For the Christian, will making is also an opportunity to testify to one's faith. From the Christian perspective, preparing our wills is basically a spiritual matter. Sadly, it has been estimated between 50% to 65% of Americans do not have a will. Such poor stewardship cannot please God. There are almost unlimited variations on the simple will, and your legal advisor will be able to assist you in determining the level of estate planning that is appropriate for you. Wills can, of course, take the form of a formal document, most often designed for you by an attorney. Upon completion that document will be notarized and signed by at least two witnesses. Another form of a will is a holographic – or handwritten – will. There are several important restrictions that apply to a handwritten will. Be aware of those restrictions for your state, and also be aware that not all states recognize the legitimacy of a handwritten will.

ESTATE PLANNING BASICS

In addition to wills, there are certain other estate planning techniques that may be effective in certain situations. Again, your attorney can provide specific guidance.

BENEFICIARY DESIGNATIONS

This is perhaps the most powerful and effective means of transferring property to another individual. Most of us are familiar with this strategy. We name beneficiaries within our life insurance policies, IRA's, 401k plans and many other type accounts. The use of a beneficiary designation is binding upon our death. Even if in our will, or our comments to family or friends, we discussed what we wanted to do or intended to do, if that property or asset is attached to a beneficiary designation, that designation is binding. This is a good example of why we routinely review our financial and estate plans to ensure they are updated in every way.

DURABLE POWER OF ATTORNEY

A power of attorney is a written document executed by one

individual authorizing another person, the "attorney-in-fact," to act on his/her behalf. Under a general power of attorney, the powers are very broad and authorize the attorney-in-fact to enter into and to discharge virtually all legal obligations on behalf of the principal. A specific power of attorney will be more limited and will authorize only specific actions on behalf of the principal. A "durable" power of attorney authorizes the attorney-in-fact to act even if the principal is incapacitated.

LIVING WILL

A Living Will is a legal document which allows an individual to state in advance his unwillingness to be subjected to life support medical measures once there is no chance of recovery. This document relieves relatives and others of the legal and emotional burden of making such decisions. The Living Will, like the Durable Power of Attorney, can be revoked at any time simply by destroying all copies of the document or by executing a signed and notarized statement revoking the prior document.

LIVING TRUST

A Living Trust (revocable) is established during lifetime and may generally be revoked or amended any time prior to death. Incompetence will render a grantor (person who places assets in the trust) incapable of revoking the trust. It should be noted that because the trust is revocable it does not have any estate tax advantages. What it does offer is the lifetime management of assets: it avoids probate, it lessens the chances for a successful challenge to the will, it provides for the prompt transfer of assets, and it can remain highly confidential. The use of the living trust is often advantageous in later years when an individual may be concerned about the management of their assets if a period of failing health and incompetency were to occur.

TRUSTS AND ARRANGEMENTS

Oliver Wendell Holmes once said, "Don't put your trust in money, put your money in trust." The use of a trust in estate planning is far too complex to cover in the pages of this book. However, you should be aware that there are distinct advantages in many cases, from the use of trusts. Some trusts can provide the means whereby estate taxes can be greatly minimized. A trust can provide for the management of assets, for the transfer of property, for the care of dependents, for special purposes, to manage a business interest, to allow for gifting, to make charitable contributions, and numerous other purposes. A trust can be said to be "testamentary," that is it is set up under the will and will not take effect until the death of the grantor. During Judy's long illness, described in the book *Goodnight, Sweetheart,* I had a testamentary trust set up within my will. Had I died before Judy, the Trust would have provided for her every need until the day of her death. On the other hand, a trust may be said to be "inter vivos," that is taking effect during the lifetime of the grantor. The grantor is the person who places assets in the trust. The assets in the trust are referred to as the "corpus" of the trust, and the "trustee" is the person or persons who has legal title to the property in the trust. These trusts are typically irrevocable, and therefore, once funded cannot be amended. Some commonly used trusts are the Marital Trust, the Residual Trust, the Life Insurance Trust, Charitable Remainder Trust, the Charitable Remainder Unitrust, the Charitable Lead Trust...and these days, many more creative and somewhat complex forms of trusts. For some, a trust will bring the satisfaction and peace of mind that their assets are protected and transferred in an efficient, effective, and amenable manner.

PURPOSE OF ESTATE PLANNING

Estate planning tends to be thought of as planning to avoid estate taxes. Surely, that is one of the functions of estate planning, but certainly not the only purpose it serves.

DISTRIBUTION

Do you have a plan as to how you would prefer to allocate your resources upon your death? There are very few options; assets can go to family and friends, charities, expenses, and taxes. With so few options the wise thing to do, the Christian thing to do, would be to have a voice in the allocation of those resources. An estate plan can be drafted to accommodate as many people and/or institutions as you would like.

CONSERVATION

It is entirely possible that an estate could lose more than half the value of that estate to federal taxes, state death taxes, administrative expenses, and probate costs. Good stewardship would seem to dictate that we establish a plan that will conserve as much of our estate as possible. The loss of assets due to lack of planning is often called "estate shrinkage." I can think of a few other terms for that loss, but I'll bite my tongue and keep those thoughts to myself. Estate taxes begin at 37% rate and extend upward to a 55% rate. That alone makes planning imperative.

ADMINSTRATION

Planning allows for the appointment of qualified and willing individuals to serve as mangers of our estates. Executors and trustees have an awesome responsibility in terms of the work that will be done when the time comes to put an estate plan into effect. These may include family members, attorneys, banks, trusted friends, and may be one, two, or even three such people or entities. You should note that by regulation executors are entitled to receive fees for their work with your estate settlement. Their job is to safeguard and manage your property, to settle debts and pay taxes during the settlement period, and ensure that remainder of the estate is passed along according to your wishes.

PROVISIONS

Provisions can be made for children, parents, spouses, and any others we choose. There are families with special situations where dependent adult children with special needs are in the home. In these cases, great care should be taken by the parents to ensure that their financial responsibilities to that dependent person are provided for, and that their wishes regarding that individual are clearly defined within their estate plan. This is one of the greatest opportunities that we have to actually "speak from the grave" for the benefit of those we love.

CONTROL

Estate planning is the avenue that is open for anyone to exercise some measure of ongoing control over their assets, even after their own death. Many situations come to mind where this control would be desirable. This would be especially true in the case of minor children, dependent adults in our care, and family members who might be spendthrifts.

CHARITABLE CAUSES

Within the Christian family, many individuals have decided that as an ongoing expression of their faith in Christ, they wish that some portion of their estate be given to their church or Christian organization. These gifts, which can be tax deductible, may be gifts made during one's lifetime or after death. Charitable gifts may be made in the form of cash, personal property, stock, appreciated assets, life insurance, annuities, real estate...in fact, the gift can be made in almost any form. Estate planning provides the format by which any believer can make a gift for the ages to the Kingdom of God.

GIFTING

Gifting, other than charitable gifting, to individuals and organizations is another component of estate planning. Current regulations permit an individual to gift $16,000 (2022) per year to as many people as they choose without incurring any gift taxes, nor will the gift count against your lifetime gift tax exclusion. This is an often-used technique to reduce estate size to avoid excessive taxation.

Organization is key to estate planning. You will want to have multiple copies of your will in safe hands and safe places. You may elect to have your named Executors have a copy, or at least to know where to access a copy. A copy, safely kept in your home, and an additional copy in a bank safety deposit box would be a good idea. Making a locator list of all vital information, including the people to contact would make work much easier for your family and others involved in the settlement of our estate. Having a will and other forms of estate planning is a privilege and a process available to all, but it is not compulsory. However, if you neglect estate planning, you can be assured that your survivors will be compelled to go into the courts and abide any decisions made on their behalf by the judge. Speak now, while you have the opportunity, so that after you are gone from this life it can be said of you, "...he still speaks, even though he is dead." The term for dying without a will is "intestate,' that is, "without one." You may have good intentions; perhaps you have even told a few people about your wishes, but those intentions and conversations will die with you. Your will, your Last Will and Testament, is that document that ensures your desires and wishes are meticulously followed.

CHAPTER 13

The Pleasure: God Loves a Cheerful Giver

I am told stories of my momma taking me to Vacation Bible School at Mt. Hebron Baptist Church in Elmore, Alabama. According to the stories I was about two years of age, and she would walk up the little dirt road, cut through the church cemetery, and hand me though the back window of the church to the ladies who were teaching the class for VBS. I share that story only to say that I have attended a Baptist church just about my entire life. For whatever you know, or think you know about Baptists, rest assured that Baptists treasure the Bible as truly the Word of God. I grew up in that rural church and was taught the Bible by some of God's finest people.

I then had the privilege to pastor some of God's finest people (and a few others too). So, I trust the Bible. I read the Bible. I study the Bible. I teach the Bible. Yet, it appears to me that there are a couple of verses related to the topic of giving that many Christians ignore, or at the very least, choose to forget.

THE TENTH BEATITUDE

The first of those verses is found in Acts 20:35, "*It is more blessed to give than to receive.*" And, if you read the verse in a red-letter edition of the Bible, you see that the verse is in red letters. That means JESUS said that!

Perhaps like me, you find something special, even soothing, every time I read the Beatitudes. After all, those words form part of the Sermon on the Mount. Can't you close your eyes and see Jesus sitting on that hillside and talking to a great throng of people, all captivated by the teaching of this man Jesus. So compelling was the teaching of Jesus that the Bible records the words of some who said of his teaching, *"We have never heard anyone teach like this."*

In Matthew 5:1-11 we find that which we call the Beatitudes. The word beatitude stems from the Latin word "beatus," which means both "happy" and "blessed." This section, the Beatitudes, is a commentary on living a blessed life, a happy life. Truthfully, Jesus intended it to constitute a call to genuine discipleship. If we understand the Beatitudes, we understand them as more than a list of blessings. Upon closer examination, we find that this lesson from Jesus defines the journey of discipleship, and he reveals that the journey of following Him leads to joy – true happiness – but the road we follow to find that blessed state is located a great distance from the road that the world (society) is traveling.

I am sure Jesus intended for us to realize that He is describing citizenship in the Kingdom. Being blessed is a matter of the heart, the soul. It is not about our surroundings; it is a function of our spirit life. The Beatitudes are not promises given to us; they are attributes of our soul as Christians. Matthew recorded these nine beatitudes as spoken by Jesus. Luke, in Acts 20:35 gives us what I choose to call the tenth beatitude, *"It is more blessed to give than to receive."* Again, this beatitude is not about a promise, it is more of a portrait of our soul. Using the old language of the KJV, Proverbs 23:7 says, *"For as he thinketh, so is he...."* Interestingly, the ESV states, *"For he is like one who is inwardly calculating."* You see, our attitudes about giving and generosity begins in our heart, and a grateful, giving heart reaps joy. In the GNT version of Proverbs 23:4 we find this, *"Be wise enough not to wear yourself out trying to get rich...."* All of this serves to remind me that the blessing that comes with giving, is reserved for the pure in heart that Jesus referenced in Matthew 5. The very essence of the Acts 20:35 blessing is found in the words of Jesus recorded in Luke 14:14, *"You will be blessed, because they cannot repay you."* How much of what we do, or what we give, is tied to what we expect to get out of the doing and giving? Remember that Proverb, *"He is like one always calculating...."* There is no blessing, no joy, not even happiness, associated with doing and giving, having determined first how it benefits me.

The Acts 20:35 text comes from Paul's visit to Ephesus and his farewell address to the elders of that church. In an equally compelling message, given to the Corinthian church, Paul further prompts our spirit to think about how we give.

SOWING AND REAPING

In 2 Corinthians 9: 7 is found this, *"Each one must give as he has decided in his heart, not reluctantly, or under compulsion, for God loves a cheerful giver."* We are not fooling God. If our heart, our attitude is not right, no amount of giving will produce the blessing and the joy that the Bible promises. Don't miss the connection between Acts 20:35 and 2 Corinthians 9:7. When was the last time you gave a significant gift to your church or to a Kingdom cause? How did it feel? Was there hesitation? Doubts? Was it done out of sense of duty? Who were you trying to impress?

The second of those verses is, of course, the verse found in 2 Corinthians 9:7, *"...for God loves a cheerful giver."* That remarkable phrase is contained in one of the most ignored and misunderstood sections of the Bible. Beginning in verse 6 and continuing through verse 15, read the verses slowly, prayerfully, reflectively. Do you hear God's voice? I do, every time I read the text.

There is a clear *message about the gift* in verse 6, a message that every farmer understands. We have come to call it the law of the harvest. A direct correlation exists between how much seed is sown and the size of the anticipated harvest. This verse begins to move us toward the realization that believers need to develop an attitude of generosity. Take another look at Philippians 4:10-20. We all love to quote verse 19, but don't miss that verse 19 is surrounded by conversation about contentment, circumstances and credits (full payment and more). It is in that context that Paul reminds us that God's supply has no shortages. Paul's message is clear: be generous.

Paul encourages us to always remember that *we have the means to give*. Paul said, *"And God is able to make all grace abound toward you, that you always having all sufficiency in all things, may have an abundance for every good work.* (NKJV) Our giving is proportional according to the supply that God has given us. When we practice grace giving, it will be generous giving. May we never forget that God spared nothing when it came to paying off our sin debt. Grace and generosity were on full display at the cross. I can't tell you what to give, but I know God expresses His *measure of a gift* based on our attitude toward operating from an abundance mentality. Our giving is like sowing seed. Paul stated that an offering is voluntary, but that does not excuse us from giving liberally, in accordance with how we are blessed. Scripture repeatedly encourages generosity:

- Proverbs 22:9 *"Whoever has a bountiful eye will be blessed, for he shares his bread with the poor."*
- Leviticus 19:10 *"You shall not strip your vineyard bare, neither shall you gather the fallen grapes of your vineyard. You shall leave them for the poor...."*
- Psalm 41:1-3 *"Blessed is the one who considers the poor! In the day of trouble the Lord delivers him; the Lord protects him and keeps him alive; he is called blessed in the land...."*

Yes, the Lord is certainly concerned with the measure of a gift, but He is equally concerned with the *motivation behind our gift*. It is here that Paul shoots with a straight arrow... *"God loves a cheerful giver."* The New Testament provides us many reminders that God looks on our hearts, reads our minds, and is not fooled by our logic or reason for any of our actions, including our giving record. I fear a few of us approach giving as though it is our dues for belonging and attending, and even for securing the favor of a church or group leader. Frankly, that "seed" will not produce a harvest.

Finally, relative to this thought, may we never fail to see God at work through the *multiplication of the gift*. The giver reaps a multiplied harvest, and the recipients are the beneficiaries of the multiplication. Paul alluded to multiplied seed and an increase in the size of the harvest.

The amazing story of the little boy with a small basket of loaves and fish seems an apt illustration. In my book *CHOSEN* I talk about the fact that Philip was the first person to hear the words, "Come follow me." Sure, others had met Jesus, but it was Philip who heard that first invitation to discipleship. Now, in chapter six of John's gospel it is to Philip that Jesus turns and asks a question, *"Where are we to buy bread so that these people might eat?"* Wow, that's a humdinger of a question. Philip, ever quick with numbers, basically replied that it would require six months of wages to feed a group that size, and based on the last treasurer's report, they did not have that kind of money in the bag. About that same time Andrew, having reconnoitered the crowd, walked into the conversation and reported having seen a little boy with a lunch basket. His report included the fact that the basket had only five barley loaves and two fish. Barley, the grain most often used by the poor, was dry and coarse – and the two fish were likely sardine-like fish which had been pickled. What circumstances...the money was insufficient, the supplies were too few, and the crowd was too large. Most of us would simply make an announcement to the folks and have them disperse and go on their way. But not Jesus. After all, His creative powers know no limits. Of Jesus, John said, *"All things were made through him, and without him was not anything made that was made."* Paul, addressing the Colossians, emphatically stated, *"For by him all things were created, in heaven and on earth, visible and invisible, whether thrones or dominions or rulers or authorities – all things were created through him and for him."* Surely, we see that our circumstances will never be an impossible challenge for His creative powers. What Philip had deemed impossible; Jesus was about to change. The miracle that ensued was the miracle of multiplication. Jesus possesses the ability to make something out of nothing, and much out of a little. Don't lose sight of the fact that in John 6:11 it was directly from the hands of Jesus that the bread and the fish were distributed to the crowd. Such miracles come from God alone. Jesus used the disciples as agents to disperse the food, but it was Jesus alone who multiplied the little basket lunch into a mass feeding project, so much so that the supply greatly exceeded the need. The miracle became possible because a little boy was willing to trust Jesus and give up his lunch. The miracle was possible because the disciples were willing to look beyond what they had and what they knew from their human perspective, in other words they cooperated with Jesus even when they did not yet fully understand all the spiritual dynamics. Not only was every person fed, but there was also more than enough. That is characteristic of how God works... *"far more abundantly than all that we ask or think, according to the power that works within us, to him be the glory...."*

ISN'T TITHING AN OLD TESTAMENT PRINCIPLE?

The concept of tithing appears throughout the Old Testament in a very clear and direct way. Most often we interpret the tithe as representing one-tenth of whatever comes into our possession. However, the tithes and offerings in Israel did not stop with the giving of one tithe, there were several tithes and many offerings. A few examples of the several tithes included the tenth of the first fruits; there was also the tenth paid by the Levites to the Priests, and there was also a second tenth paid by the entire congregation for the needs of the Levites and their families, and there was a fourth tithe for the poor, which was paid every third year. But what does all of this have to do with Christians and the church today? It is apparent that Paul taught something well beyond the tithe, he taught grace giving, and if we are honest, we immediately recognize that early churches were taught – and practiced – giving out of their abundance of joy. In 2 Corinthians 8:2 Paul says of the Christians in Macedonia, "for *in a severe test of affliction, their abundance of joy and their extreme poverty have overflowed in a wealth of generosity on their part. For they gave according to their means, as I can testify, and beyond their means, of their own accord....*" The Christians gave well outside the boundaries of the tithe. Why would so many, who had so little, give so much? It's simple.... because of their love for the Lord. So many of the conversations about tithes and offerings in our churches results in weeping, and wailing, and gnashing of teeth. Why do you suppose that is? Consider what Paul said in 2 Corinthians 8:2 about the attitude of those Macedonian givers. It said, *"And this, not as we expected, but they gave themselves first to the Lord and then by the will of God to us."* Those believers were worshippers and seekers of God, and they saw their giving not as being forced or manipulated into giving, rather they did it as an act of worship and fellowship. In other words, our giving demonstrates the level of our love for Christ. We have already discussed the fact that the Bible teaches us that God loves a hilarious giver. Offering time in most churches is too somber, certainly absent any outbursts of laughter. Given the attitude of a few, we might mistake the offering time in some churches for an invitation to visit the wailing wall in Jerusalem.

Sure, there always seems to be at least one person who invariably says, "But that is the Old Testament, and we are not under the law." My initial internal reaction to that thinking is this simple question, "Okay, what are we trying to excuse or exempt ourselves from relative to Scripture?" This is not the place for an exhaustive discourse on the theological significance of what Jesus said in Matthew 5:17-20 about his relationship to the law. He identified himself as not the replacement, but the fulfillment of the law. And yes, we operate under the Grace of God, not the Law of God. At the same time James 1:17 says, *"I the Lord do not change."* God is not evolving. God is not still in the learning phase of his existence. God is not increasing, or diminishing for that matter, in power and knowledge. He was, and is, and is to come, eternal in every attribute. His very essence, along with his knowledge, understanding and character are not up for debate. There are a number of theological places in which I agree with the reformers, and this is one of them – that nothing has changed, nor will it change, in regard to God's moral law. Clearly, God punishes sin and rewards goodness. The entirety of the book of Malachi is the story of God's loving pursuit, lavish provisions and lasting promises. But it is also the story of obstinate people who appear indifferent toward, if not ignorant of, the ongoing blessings of God. In the second verse in the prophetic book God said, *"I have loved you."* What a statement! Yet, seven times in this short book the people replied, *"How have you loved us?"* That question, and the attitude behind it, had the nation of Israel in upheaval. I mean, they were in a "messed up" place politically, morally, socially, philosophically and spiritually. Don't forget, after Malachi's prophetic message – and the lack of moral change – it would be four hundred years before Israel would once again hear a word from God. Are we in danger of losing the blessings of God, just as did Israel?

Surely, we can agree that the moral law of God is not evolving. To that end, cannot we not also agree that it is immoral to steal? It is both interesting and important to see the divine connection to Malachi's treatise on tithing and the moral collapse of a nation. In chapter three the prophet begins with a question regarding morality. *"Will a man rob God?"* Only the vilest and most depraved would be so stupid to steal from God. Yet, that was Malachi's indictment of Israel. So perhaps we would be better served if we paid more attention to the intent of God's message and less time debating over the validity of tithing. After all, we appear to have a few curses lingering around us, just as did those early Israelites. Could our giving and generosity decisions have an impact on the future course of our families and our nation?

Perhaps we find at least part of our answer in Malachi 3:9, *"You are under a curse – the whole nation of you – because you are robbing me."*

A Curse...

The Return - In verse seven of Malachi 3 we get a glimpse of a pattern that existed in the life of the Jewish people. This is found in the fact that the Lord calls them a rebellious people. In fact, in the verse God reminded them that they had been a nation of rebellious people since the day of their forefathers. The history of Israel had moved in a cycle...they became affluent and forgot God, then justice comes, and they suffer; then they repent and experience the forgiveness of God. It was evident in Abraham, who in danger, pretended his wife to be his sister and in so doing was failing to trust God for protection. It was evident in Jacob who deceived his father and cheated his brother out of the family birthright. Again, it is seen in Exodus 16 as an ungrateful nation murmured against God. Then there was the incident in 1 Samuel when Israel wanted to be like other nations and demanded that God allow them to have a king. Do you see a pattern yet? Surely you do! There was no denying it, they were a rebellious people.

We might expect God to immediately lash out at the sin, the ingratitude, the evil...however, we find instead that the Lord issued a plea. *"Return to me and I will return to you"* was the challenge issued to Israel. We might say this was a call to repentance. But isn't that just like

God? There He is giving us opportunities that we don't deserve. The preaching of John the Baptist, Jesus, and Simon Peter in the gospels and Acts were messages calling all of us to repentance. The very opportunity to repent is an extension of the mercy of God.

It is also important to take note of the fact that along with the plea, God also issued a promise. His promise to Israel was that if they would return to Him, He would return to them. I think if nothing else, this text provides us with the evidence that Jehovah desires fellowship with His people and that He grieves when we stray. Unfortunately, we also see the passiveness of Israel, for in verse seven they ask the question, "...*how shall we return?*" In other words, they were saying, "We've done nothing wrong, why should we repent? We don't see anything wrong with the way things are right now." What a commentary on our present day. We are no longer just drifting away from God and the foundations of morality and rightness upon which this country was built, we are racing away from God at break-neck speed. Sadly, the majority, like the Israelites see nothing wrong with the way things are.

The Robbery - We come quickly to the crux of the problem that has brought about this curse in verse eight, "*Will a man rob God? Yet you rob me. But you ask, how do we rob you? In tithes and offerings. You are under a curse-the whole nation of you-because you are robbing me.*" God laid the charge at their feet quickly; they were not paying their tithes and were therefore guilty of robbery. The Lord emphatically states in Leviticus 27 that the tithe belongs to the Lord. The Bible says that everything that comes into our possession, should be tithed upon.

What happens if we fail in that regard? Verse nine clearly says that a curse will befall those who ignore this command of God. I contend that the shortages that we are currently experiencing have a direct link to our neglect of God's economic principles. Where did we ever get the notion that God made giving optional? Where did we get the idea that we could ignore His word and not experience the consequences of our abuse and neglect of His principles. I believe there are believers today who are experiencing shortages and courting economic disaster because they have chosen to ignore this command. What exactly had this curse meant to Israel? We are told in the text that pests were devouring their fields, their crops were spoiling in the field, and their fruit was rotting on the trees. To an agrarian society, that was totally devastating to their economy. Hmm, sounds familiar.

In verse 10 we see a command that is two-fold. First there is the command to tithe. We are to do that by bringing the tithe, the tenth part, into the storehouse. I believe the storehouse is the church, and I therefore believe that is where the tithe belongs. Gifts that we make beyond the tithe might be directed elsewhere to Kingdom causes, but the tithe belongs in the church. The second part of the command is found in the words, *"Test me in this, says the Lord Almighty..."* The blessing of God awaits those who accept at face value this challenge to take the tithe, put it in the storehouse, and trust God to provide for our needs. It has been my personal experience that the ninety percent has a way of going longer and farther than the one hundred percent when I have tried to hoard it all for myself.

The Receiving - So now what? I've obeyed God, I've given the tithe, what happens now? The Lord has answered that for you in verse ten, *"...and see if I will not throw open the floodgates of heaven and pour out so much blessing that you will not have room enough to receive it."* We see here the source of our blessing is God Himself. There is nothing in the way of supply that has not come from God. We also see here the scope of the blessing. Nothing will be held back. The vaults of heaven will be opened and so great will be the flow that we will not even be capable of comprehending the blessing of God. Paul said in Ephesians 3:20-21, *"Now to him who is able to do immeasurably more than all we ask or imagine, according to his power that is at work with us, to him be glory in the church and in Christ Jesus throughout all generations, for ever and ever! Amen."*

The Rebuke - When we are obedient in this matter of the tithe the Lord moves into action on our behalf. He is going to rebuke the devourer, lift the curse, and prosperity will follow. He will be our defense against that which could devour our ability to get in on the flow of God. Our lack, our shortages, can usually be linked to some violation of a precept of God. Ask Him to show you where you may have erred, then confess it and correct it and then expect the windows of heaven to open on you.

A Commitment...

Clearly, God made a commitment (open the windows of heaven), and he expected a commitment from those hearing from the prophet (to be generous). Generally, in the churches I have served and attended, we do not solicit pledges for the general budget. We have certainly done that for special campaigns such as buildings, etc. I certainly see nothing wrong with asking congregations to make giving pledges. People sign on the "dotted line" for thirty-year mortgages, and these days five- and six-year car loan payments. But let's face it, commitment begins within our hearts, our souls. God's economic plan rests on a plan of keeping resources in circulation. That does not dismiss the need to plan and prepare for the future. But it does mean that our planning should include, both now and when I am gone, giving that blesses others – and it also means being generous in the here and now. God is in the business of meeting needs and supplying resources to meet our needs, and most often God elects to do that through people. That means I am to be a conduit for both giving and receiving. I began two businesses before I was twelve years told, and I had been taught as a child to tithe, and therefore tithed and gave offerings from those meager earnings. By age thirteen I began working in a country general store. I was paid $3.00 per day for a job that began at 7:00 a.m. and ended at 7:00 p.m. – and yes, I tithed on those earnings. And even then, I still saved money (in an old cigar box) that allowed me to buy baseball gloves, a bicycle and eventually my first car. That is still ingrained in my spirit today, and I believe it is one of the most basic of all spiritual disciplines. Do I feel compelled to tithe? Yes, but not by any church, rather by God himself, and obey I must.

The Collection...

"Oh brother, here we go, another collection at the church." Perhaps you've never said it, but I imagine that you have probably at least thought it. Perhaps you sometimes feel that the church is costly, just a big depository for all those offerings that are taken every Sunday.

A man was once heard complaining, "Our church costs too much." A friend replied, "Let me tell you a story. Sometime ago a little boy was born in our home...he cost us a lot from the beginning. There was formula, food, clothes, medicine, etc. to buy. Then he went to school, and that cost us even more, and then there was college, and that cost us a small fortune. Then our boy died...and after his funeral expenses were paid, he hasn't cost us another cent. Now which situation do you think we would prefer?"

The church is alive and has the most vital message in the world and does many things and provides many things that we take for granted. It takes resources to provide ministries that meet people at the point of their need. If the church were to die, it would be greatly missed and we would all likely say, "I'll do my part to keep it alive." Well, the church is alive, and we have an opportunity to do our part. An old preacher was once heard to say, "Three books are necessary for the church, the good book; the hymn book; and the pocketbook." I have used that often, and no argument has yet changed my mind as to its accuracy.

Paul in the I Corinthians 16 passage gives us some principles concerning the offering of the church that we must not forget.

Giving Should Be Punctual....

Paul said that we are to bring our offering on the first day of the week. In the New Testament the first day of the week quickly became the accepted and practiced day of worship, being linked to the resurrection of Christ. The early church did many things on the first day of the week. They fellowshipped on that day, they preached on that day, they worshipped, they sang...and they gave their tithes and offerings. God in His wisdom knew that we would need some system, for without it we would remain undisciplined and irregular in our worship and giving. So, he ordered that the first day of the week would be a time for the church to gather for worship...to preach, to sing and to collect an offering.

Giving Should Be Personal....

Paul left no one out, he said, *"let every one of you lay by him in store...*In the NIV it says, *"...each one of you should set aside a sum of* *money....*" This involves everyone: old, young, rich, poor. This statement means that no one is too poor to give. "Lay by in store" is an interesting phrase. It means to "treasure up a precious thing." It reminds us of Mary's expensive perfume. No wonder she treasured it, for it cost her a year's wages. Her friends had probably encouraged her many times to use the fragrance. "Why, it smells too good to sit in the container." But she refused, stating that she was saving it for something special. Jesus was that something special and the perfume became her love gift to Him. Our offering needs to be our love gift to Jesus, more than the hurried scribbling of a check. It ought to be an act of personal worship.

Giving Should Be Proportional....
Paul said, "*...each one of you should set aside a sum of money in keeping with his income.*" Take note of the fact that this offering that Paul was asking for was beyond their regular tithe and offering. The Jews gave a tithe without question...but they did not stop there. They gave other offerings as well, often as much as twenty to thirty percent of their income. Giving is to be proportional, that is, as God has prospered us. Paul has left this matter of the offering open to the reasonableness of the Christian. Surely, in Christ, we have been blessed so, so much - and our giving should reflect the measure of our gratitude.

Giving meets God's expectation and is an expression of thanksgiving on our part. It is the means ordained by God to meet the needs of those around us. Our disobedience in the matter can bring the devourer, the curse. Our obedience will truly open the windows of heaven. What can, and will you do today to practice generosity?

STEWARDSHIP

I want to recommend two books, both of which will help provide some Biblical truth and perspective on Christian stewardship. Many years ago, while attending a training class led by Ron Blue, I met Ken Boa. I have remained on his mailing list for his monthly thought provoking, heart stirring, Holy Spirit inspired publication, *Reflections,* from his Reflections Ministries organization. Ken is the co-author of the two books I am passing along with hope that you will read them. The title of the first book is *Leverage: Using Temporal Wealth for Eternal Gain.* This book discusses the why and how of giving now versus waiting until we die. The book presents four reasons that current giving versus delayed giving can make so much sense. The authors refer to giving now instead of later as, "giving with a warm hand rather than a cold hand." The book provides a magnificent comparison of our stewardship of both financial and spiritual capital. *Recalibrate Your Life* is the second book. It was this book that caused me to take a much more exhaustive approach to my understanding of my role as a steward. Boa uses the three T's that we have long used to define the boundaries of our stewardship responsibilities: time, talent and treasure.

Too often we think time is in short supply, but it is not, it is simply that I have at times been a poor steward of time. In another part of this book, I talk about the many words in the Bible that are translated as "time." I must confess that there are times (opportunities) that I wish I could "do-over." Most of us have complained that we wish we had more time. Frankly, we have all the time we need; we just need to become better stewards of that time.

How about your talent (natural, spiritual, acquired)? Are you maximizing who and what you are in Christ? Genuine fulfillment comes only when we are using all our talents in God-honoring tasks and time.

The third T (treasure) is what so much of this book is about. Money. I just glanced at the calendar, and I have only 34 days remaining before I am accountable to the IRS for reporting my annual income and determining if I have paid all the imposed taxes. My lack of stewardship in that area comes with costly penalties. As I wrote earlier, our lack of stewardship before God can also carry a cost. It is this matter of stewarding our treasure that seems to trouble us most. Our money, our wealth, our resources can bring blessings, but those same resources can bring many challenges.

I am adding a fourth T – the stewardship of thoughts. Jesus said that what we say, is what comes from our heart (mind). Proverbs 23:7 makes the connection between our thinking and our actions. Paul reminds us of the need to take certain thoughts captive. The stewardship of my thoughts includes managing my diet – not of food – but what I read, what I watch, what I listen to...it matters. We have all heard an individual brag, "Well, I just speak my mind." I can think many snappy, curt replies to that notion, but that is not my point. When the angel revealed to the virgin Mary that she was going to give birth to the Christ child, the Bible says she *"treasured up all these things, pondering them in her heart."* That's stewardship of her thoughts. Paul provides us with an excellent thought stewardship plan, *"...whatever is true, whatever is honorable, whatever is just, whatever is commendable, if there is any excellence, if there is anything worthy of praise, think about these things."*

The fifth T I have chosen to call the stewardship of touches. As I think about all the individuals that have "crossed my path" in these more than seven decades it causes me to take inventory of what difference, if any, have I made in those lives. That inventory becomes increasingly important as I evaluate the relationships with the close circle of friendships I have, and again, even more so with family. Our encounters with others do matter. Are those lives in any way changed? Were there outcomes that were positively impacted? Did they know how much I cared, how much I loved? Do I pray for them? Have I been the hands and feet of Jesus as was needed? God expects us to be good stewards of all our relationships.

The final T on my list is the responsibility to be a steward of the truth. Sadly, our society and culture has arrived at a moment in time when truth is in short supply. Disinformation and misinformation have become the norm. We cannot trust the media. We have learned that we cannot trust our own government. We suddenly have a long list of professionals – lawyers, doctors, CEO's, politicians, business owners, and even some church and religious leaders – who, through coverups, manipulation, distortion, exaggeration, fabrication, omission – make a regular practice of untruthfulness. As Christians, we above all others, need to be – no, we must be – agents of all that is true and right. Truth must never be compromised for what is convenient or expedient. Truth is truth! America is currently in a draught, a famine, a war, relative to truthfulness. Jesus boldly stated, *"The truth will set you free."* That statement brings to my recall a statement once made by Abraham

Lincoln, *"I am not bound to win, but I am bound to be true. I am not bound to succeed, but I am bound to live up to what light I have."* Lincoln also espoused a belief in the American people who, if given the real facts, can be depended on to do the right thing. He went on to say, *"The great point is to give them the real facts."* How is it possible for a lie (anything short of the truth) to find its way into a church, or any Christian's heart. I think Jesus provided our answer in John 16:13, *"When the Spirit of truth comes, he will guide you into all truth...."* Anytime a believer – including Pastors and leaders – speak anything that is not based on truth it is clear evidence that they are operating from the "flesh" and not the "Spirit." Jesus bluntly said, *"I am the way, and the truth, and the life...."* He went on to say, in His great prayer for believers, *"Sanctify them in the truth; your word is truth."* Sanctify means to "set apart." We Christians are set apart from the world around us, and in Colossians the Apostle Paul goes through a list of all that Christians need to "put off" and "put on." He states that we must put off any and all things associated with a life outside of Jesus Christ. There are no half-truths in the Bible, it is either true, or it's a lie. No preacher or teacher has the authority to operate outside the bounds of Scripture. God is unchanging, and so is His word. In Ephesians chapter six we are given a list of the armor that we have for living an upright and God pleasing life – by resisting and waging war against the devil – by suiting up for the fight. In the list of armor this is included, *"Stand therefore, having fastened on the belt of truth...."* The devil is called, in the Bible, "the father of all lies," and here we learn how God has equipped us to live in the truth, and to speak the truth.

As we digest what the Bible teaches us about the matter of stewardship, may we remember that the very word stewardship reminds us that we own (possess) nothing, we are simply entrusted with the management of what belongs to God. In Luke 16:1-13 is the parable of Jesus about the unjust steward – or, as the ESV refers to him, the dishonest manager. Our management (stewardship) of our God given resources is important enough that Jesus spoke often and plainly about our faithful execution of our responsibility to manage all of God's resources. May we never forget, God takes pleasure in all that we do in His name.

CHAPTER 14

The Perspective: Learning to Balance Life

What does that even mean? Living a balanced life? I found a myriad of thoughts as to what some mean by the notion of maintaining a balanced lifestyle. One source suggested that "Lifestyle balance occurs when you establish a healthy mixture of the different domains of living." Yes, but doesn't that sound overly academic? I read another article that provided a list of steps to take to attain a more balanced life. Gee, if I must add seven more steps to my already busy life doesn't that just make it more complicated? One writer suggested that I just needed to do all I could to "make myself happy." Good luck with that one. The World Health Organization (WHO), and who doesn't trust them, states with utmost certainty that a balanced and healthy lifestyle is defined as "a state of complete physical, mental and social well-being." Well, sounds good to me...but "How?" remains the question. Perhaps the Bible is a good place to find that answer.

SCRIPTURE

There is ample evidence from the Bible to confirm that God wants us to live a balanced life. Scripture affirms the need to maintain a healthy balance for the sake of our mind, body and spirit.

Ecclesiastes 3: 1-8 *"There is a time for everything, and a season for every activity under the heavens: a time to be born, and a time to die, a time to plant and a time to uproot, a time to kill and a time to heal, a time to tear down and a time to build, a time to weep and a time to laugh, a time to mourn and a time to dance, a time to scatter stones and a time to gather them, a time to embrace and a time to refrain from embracing, a time to search and a time to give up, a time to keep and a time to throw away, a time to tear and a time to mend, a time to be silent and a time to speak, a time to love and a time to hate, a time for war and a time for peace.* (NIV)

Matthew 6: 31-34 *"Therefore, do not be anxious saying, what shall we eat, what shall we wear? But seek first the kingdom of God and his righteousness, and all these things will be added unto you. Therefore, do not be anxious for tomorrow, for tomorrow will be anxious for itself..."*

1 Corinthians 6: 19-20 *"Do you not know that your body is a temple of the Holy Spirit within you, whom you have from God? You are not your own, for you were bought with a price, so glorify God in your body."*

Philippians 4: 8 *"Finally, brothers and sisters, whatever is noble, whatever is right, whatever is pure, whatever is lovely, whatever is admirable – if anything is excellent or praiseworthy – think about such things."* (NIV)

Romans 12:2 *"Do not conform to the pattern of this world, but be transformed by the renewing of your mind. Then you will be able to test and approve what God's will is – his good, pleasing and perfect will."* (NIV)

Philippians 4: 11-12 *"I am not saying this because I am in need, for I have learned to be content whatever the circumstances. I know how to be in need, and I know what it is to have plenty. I have learned the secret of being content in every situation...."* (NIV)

1 Peter 5: 7 *"Casting all your anxieties on him, because he cares for you."*

Ephesians 5:29 *"After all, no one ever hated their own body, but they feed and care for their body, just as Christ does the church..."* (NIV)

Ephesians 4:32 *"Be kind and compassionate to one another...."* (NIV)

Hebrews 13:5 *"Keep your life free from the love of money, and be content with what you have, for he has said, 'I will never leave you nor forsake you'...the Lord is my helper."*

I could continue to quote the many, many Bible references to the sanctity of our lives – mind, body and spirit. It was God's original plan that we enjoy the presence of God, enjoy work, and enjoy the fruits and benefits that come from living in harmony with God and His creation. The events in Eden changed that script. Now, many of us try to live without God, and consequently we have a void in our mind, body and spirit that nothing outside of a relationship with God can mend. But, just as the events in Eden changed the script, so it is that the conquest on Calvary forever changed the script. Romans 8:22-28 proclaims the change: *"For we know that the whole creation has been groaning together... and not only creation, but we ourselves....we wait eagerly for the adoptions as sons, the redemption of our bodies. For in this hope we were saved... likewise the Spirit helps us in our weakness...and we know that for those who love God all things work together for good, for those who are called according to his purpose...to be conformed to the image of his Son."* When aligned, God's plan and our perspective result in blended, bountiful blessings.

STORIES

Here are three stories that relate to the issue of misplaced priorities, and a warped perspective of how God views our pursuit of wealth. Don't misunderstand, the Bible does not condemn wealth nor those who have wealth. It is our personal thinking and our individual actions relative to wealth that brings us to hard and broken places. I have often heard 1 Timothy 6:10 misquoted (money is the root of all evil). You and I know what it actually says: *"For the love of money is the root of all evil."* In other words, it is our perspective toward and with money that can become the problem. Jesus told several stories that address this very issue, in fact the first one reports an actual encounter Jesus had with a very fine young man.

The Rich Young Ruler

Most of us are very familiar with this story – which is recorded in three of the gospels – and tells the story of a young man who approached Jesus. We have long referred to him as the rich young ruler. No single account of his encounter with Jesus refers to him as such, but Matthew does tell us he was young, and Luke tells us he was a ruler. All three of the gospels imply he had wealth. Using Matthew 19:16-22, we drop in and listen to the conversation that Jesus had with the young man, and with select disciples. His story begins with the *question of salvation*. In fact, the question of salvation comes up twice in this same context. First, the young man asked, "What must I do to be saved?" Later, the disciples, after having heard the conversation with the young man asked Jesus, "Who then can be saved?" There is no more important question that anyone could ask. Clearly, he approached Jesus clinging to the concept of a religion of works. His question was both presumptuous and preposterous. "What must I do to be saved?"

I have spent too much of my life on what "I" can do, how about you? Oh, I fully understand that I can do nothing to earn or merit salvation. But many of us, in our religious and spiritual lives continue to focus on what we can do, as if we can substitute activity at church for abiding with Christ. Such a predilection comes from a warped perception of God. The young man came with a distorted view of Christ. Yes, he called him a good teacher, and even some among the religious elite were willing to admit that he was a good teacher. Yet Jesus challenged him on his definition of good. I have had that conversation with the Lord many times, and most often when I am honest with God, my good and his best are not the same. The young man also approached Jesus with a distorted view of sin. Wow, we certainly reside in a world which has a distorted view of sin. It's not that some of the evil that we see on the streets did not exist in the past, but it has leaped from the shadows onto Main Street and, thanks to the media, straight into our living rooms. The young man was indeed a good person – moral, upright, law abiding, highly religious, good at heart. But, when he looked in a mirror, he did not see a sinner. Jesus looked beyond the veneer of the good man that he was and saw that the young man was a victim of his own greed. His great sin was being covetous. When Jesus confronted that issue the young man flinched. When Jesus asked him to sell what he had – not in order to earn or buy salvation – Jesus was asking him to do something a covetous person would never do. Like many people, including the Jews of his day, the rich young ruler had a distorted view of salvation. Like so many, he wanted salvation on his terms, not God's.

That thought brings us to the *question of surrender.* The young man asked, "What do I lack?" Here we quickly see his perspective on life was attached to what he owned. Jesus reply to the question was "Sell what you have and give it to the poor." Behind the exterior of goodness was a heart that worshipped possessions, and Jesus knew that about him. You see, it is impossible to love God with all our heart and hold even one thing back. The young man's departure was sad on many levels. At some point I read or heard it said, this young man appears to be the only person in the Bible who approached Jesus and went away worse than he came. The story closes with a final question, this one from his disciples, it was the *question about sacrifice.* Hearing the conversation between Jesus and the young man apparently got some of them thinking, and likely talking among themselves. Ever the one most inclined to speak first, Peter asked, "What shall we have?" Another way of saying that is, "What's in it for me?" Is that your approach in your relationship with Christ? Is that your question about your church? If so, pray that God reshapes your perspective on what it means to follow Jesus.

The Rich Fool

Found in Luke 12:13:21 is a parable told by Jesus. The message at the heart of the parable is not about how much we might own, but the question of how much of us is owned by the stuff we have, and the stuff we want. In my study there is a plaque – made by the son of a dear lady I had the privilege of serving as teacher and pastor – it reads, "God doesn't care how much stuff you have...He cares how much stuff has you."

Again, this chapter is about perspective and how our perspective influences our pursuits. Most people think of the Ten Commandments as a list of heinous sins, sins that are a reproach to God and man. Yet, there is one of those commandments that, at least based on our perception, is not so bad after all. Based on what we think, say and do, many of us stop reading after the ninth commandment, for number ten begins with these words, *"You shall not covet...."* This man whom Jesus called a fool certainly violated that commandment. He stood gazing at what he had accomplished, what he had earned, what he had acquired – and wanted a little more. A story that persists about John D. Rockefeller involves his reply to a question about how much money is enough. The story says that his reply was, "just a little bit more." At the time he owned 90% of all the oil and gas production in the U.S. Our man in Luke 12 epitomizes that perspective. Just a little bit more. He even said it: "I will tear down my barns and build bigger barns." As we are all prone to do, the man made a *grand estimate* of his life. Notice in verse 16 that all his thoughts were turned inward. No consideration of God. No consideration of others. Proudly he repeated "I will," "I will," "I will," "I will." Proud of himself he said, *"Self, you've done well! You've got it made and can now retire. Take it easy and have the time of your life!"* (MSG) Again, from the Message Bible, the next phrase says, *"Just then God showed up and said, 'Fool,' Tonight you die. And your barnful of goods- who gets them?"* The man had made a grand estimate of his life's accomplishments and all he had acquired, but he made a *grave error*. In his accountant's books he was wealthy and set for life, but his error was that he had forgotten that it is God who "owns the cattle on a thousand hills", and it is in celebration of God that "all of the trees clap their hands," and it is to God that "the rocks cry out" in praise. God owns and controls it all. He said the "gold and the silver are mine."

May we never, as did this rich fool, make the mistake of thinking that we have done anything apart from the grace and favor of God. For the rich fool, it was a grave error. Such thoughts and actions can lead to unwanted consequences. Certainly, for this man, the outcome was a *ghastly ending*. It is likely that he went to bed on that last night thinking he would rise the next morning and go about his affairs as he had for all the days before. But, for this farmer, it all ended that night, and his entire life was summed up in one word: "Fool." A fool can be one who acts imprudently, unwise. The farmer was certainly that person. But a fool can also be defined as one who has been deceived. No doubt, everyone in the community – including all the other farmers – deemed him a success. But not God. God saw instead a man who had been deceived by the allure of accolades, achievement and accumulation. In

Luke 16, Jesus told another story about a rich man who lived only for himself. Upon death that rich man was reminded that a great chasm existed between his place of existence and that of others. In both instances we have stories of how the gnawing appetite for more and more can separate us from God and those we love. The story in Luke 12 closes with Jesus making a statement to his disciples regarding the *great emptiness* that comes from wrong pursuits and perceptions. Jesus said, *"I tell you, don't be anxious about your life, what you will eat, nor about your body, what you will put on it. For life is more than food and the body more than clothing... your Father knows what you need... instead, seek His kingdom, and these things will be added to you."* (Luke 12:22-31)

GET IT RIGHT!

Remember Hezekiah? He was a great King – he loved God and led an entire nation in a spiritual awakening and revival...and yet, to such a good person, one who had done many good things, righteous things, God said, *"Get your house in order."* Eventually we all come to that place, the place where this life is left behind and we step into eternity. If anything is missing, or misaligned in your life, it's time to get it right. Are your priorities aligned with those of God? Get it right.

CHAPTER 15

The Preparation: Parents – Children – Widows

In this chapter we will deal with two critical areas of focus in financial planning. The first is to help parents make the connection between family values and money. Such teaching begins when children are very young, perhaps coaching them around their young exuberance to spend their entire allowance on a single item, or at least consider saving something for another day. Better they learn such concepts while young before habits become ingrained in their young minds. The second area requiring forethought and preparation is what happens when we lose a loved one, or a marriage dissolves. The Bible makes many references to the need to pay special attention to widows. There is also the escalating rate of divorce, even among Christians. Such circumstances will often require complex financial and legal considerations, all of which can be confusing and cumbersome to navigate. My hope is that this brief chapter at least creates some healthy conversations within households and families.

Children and Parents.... Relative to children, many issues grab the attention of every parent. We previously discussed the need for preparation and planning beginning at an early age. The world of finance has greatly changed since I was a child, and as we can all attest, the changes occur in rapid-fire order. Perhaps there is no greater change than the explosion of digital options replacing the use of cash. I received a small allowance as a child and I began working to earn money by the time I was ten years old, and by age thirteen I had an after school and weekend job. I saved my money in an old cigar box. At age fifteen I bought my first car, using money from that cigar box. At age sixteen I became a bit more sophisticated by opening an account at the First National Bank of Wetumpka, AL. I continued using the cigar box for "ready cash," and the bank for savings. I remember just before the start of my sophomore year in high school, my friend Bobby Joe and I rode the bus to Montgomery. With our pockets full of money that we had earned, we walked up and down Dexter Avenue buying shirts, socks and jeans for school. Today I see teens using debit and credit cards – provided by their parents — to buy not only clothes but the latest in digital devices. And they drive away in expensive automobiles. I bring this up only because it causes me to ask an internal question, "What values are we teaching our children about money, spending and generosity?" I was once reminded (wish I could remember who) that while our thinking is unconscious – we don't remember actual thoughts – we do remember the words attached to our thoughts. To that end parents could begin at an early age to help their children develop a money values vocabulary. We parents could do a much better job of reinforcing good money habits making statements that express and explain what is important to us relative to how we use money. Statements that express family values, clarify the value of meaningful work, emphasize the need for long-term thinking and planning, and of course, basic issues of responsibility that are critical in raising financially literate and socially adjusted children. I learned the value of "dignity in honest work" from my dad, and the value of relationships from both my parents. Respect for others and their property was a value both spoken and demonstrated by my parents. I might change the lyrics to an old Pete Seeger song to sound like this...

> *Where have all the values gone?*
> *Long time passing.*
> *Where have all the values gone?*

Long time ago.
Where have all the values gone?
The parents forgot them everyone.
Oh, when will you ever learn?
Oh, when will you ever learn?

There is another line in that song that provides an answer to a rhetorical question about soldiers, and that line is sobering, *"They've gone to graveyards everyone."* Mounting national and personal debt, unhealthy, excessive lifestyles, a sense of entitlement, a disdain for work and capitalism – all suggest that many important values have made their way to the graveyard.

Talk and teaching around values-based financial decisions can produce long lasting results with children. Key issues for such conversations could include sacrifice versus instant-gratification, self-worth versus self-fulfillment and guarding against excess are relevant and needful. Children are likely to learn more from we parents by what they see versus what they hear. In Exodus 34:7 is an oft misquoted and misunderstood verse. It says, *"...visiting the iniquity of the fathers upon the children, and the children's children..."* The line appears in a work of Shakespeare as well. That verse is about the consequences that can linger from past decisions and actions. God is in the sin forgiving business, and when we ask for forgiveness, we find it. Yet, forgiveness does not always imply that the consequences of an action are abated. So yes, our children are likely to learn, and continue to emulate, what they see in their parents.

If you are looking for help in formulating financial plans that can reflect your personal and spiritual values, you might consider seeking counsel from a financial professional who is a member of "Kingdom Advisors." I became a member when it was still known as Christians Financial Professionals Network. Kingdom Advisors, as an organization, is committed to delivering biblical financial wisdom to their clients. Those advisors can help integrate your faith into your financial plan.

Teaching children how to think about and how to handle money is a neglected, if not forgotten, task assigned to parents. The Bible makes it clear that we must teach character to our children while they are young. Proverbs 22:6 affirms that by stating, *"Train up a child in the way he should go; even when he is old, he will not depart from it."* You see, the problem with money is not really about money, the heart of the problem is typically a values issue. If we are not careful, we will teach our children, or allow them to be taught by society, that we are defined by how much or how little money we have. We live in a culture that defines self-worth by net worth. Such a notion is foreign to the Bible. Scripture dictates that we as parents develop character within our children that values who we are, not what we have. The world operates with an attitude that demands instant gratification. The Bible (Philippians 4:11), on the other hand, teaches us about contentment. The world teaches us to grab all we can and hold on to it. The Bible, on the other hand, says God owns everything (Psalm 24:1). The Bible shows us the wisdom of systematically saving and investing in order to grow wealth over time. (Proverbs 13:11; 28:20) The world, like lemmings over the side of a cliff, keeps falling for the next get rich quick scheme. While the world grabs and hoards, the Bible teaches generosity (Proverbs 22:9). Often the world, with a stubborn and stingy value system, says it is all about me and mine, and I will do it my way. On the other hand, the Bible reminds us that the wise seek good counselors. (Proverbs 12:15) The American culture into which I write this book has become a society of takers, with few givers. Employers can't find enough employees. How did our nation arrive at such a place? Workers are missing in action. Why? That philosophy was learned somewhere, but certainly not from the Bible. Proverbs 28:19 says, *"Whoever works his land will have plenty of bread, but he who follows worthless pursuits will have plenty of poverty."*

Let's set some realistic expectations for preparing our children to be healthy and wise in their use of all things financial. Unfortunately, most teens leave high school as financial illiterates. For many years I volunteered with Junior Achievement, an organization that introduces students to on-grade-level financial and business concepts. I always volunteered for the elementary grade level classes. By the time students reach high school, if financial wisdom has not passed through their parents, it is likely that they have developed many bad money habits and values. Most students leave high school without ever learning how to maintain a balance sheet (Can you say "checkbook"?) of their personal finances. I am reminded of a time when my youngest daughter was a preschooler, and she was with me shopping in some store. She spotted something she wanted, and I replied that I did not have enough money to buy the item. Her age four-year-old reply was, "Well, Daddy, just write a check." At age four it must have seemed to her that somehow there was always an endless supply of money on the other end of those checks. We must never waste those teachable moments.

Consider these age-level teaching opportunities:

Preschoolers – As I mentioned in the incident with my four-year-old daughter, shopping affords a wonderful way to begin teaching children the concept of money. Frankly, with the advent of so many digital forms of making transactions I think we have lost a marvelous teaching opportunity with the use of loose change (coins) and currency. I am amazed how many teenagers whom I encounter at a cash register don't have a clue as to how to make change...and sometimes even with the register making the calculation for them.

Elementary school – By now we should have been teaching our children not only about how money is exchanged, but we should have begun the process of instilling in them that all our resources come from God, and that we need to be generous in giving back to God. I can remember learning to save money – earned by my efforts, gifted by grandparents, birthday money – in order to have enough to purchase something I really, really wanted. My parents gave me an old cigar box and that box became my personal banking system. For years to come I bought baseball gloves, a bicycle – and eventually as a teenager – even bought my first car with money I saved up in that cigar box. By, the way, although my money today is in banks and brokerage firms, I still have that cigar box. That cigar box taught me many valuable lessons – delayed gratification, how to shop for value, how to negotiate, and, how to make decisions about what really mattered. Larry Burkett used to teach couples to take envelopes and put cash in those envelopes to ensure they had the money to pay bills and pay off debts. Perhaps you could develop such a system for your kids.

Middle school – I was working in a general store when I was this age. Growing up, as I did, in a small country village, I began working in the store by the time I was in the sixth grade. During the summer I worked a regular schedule, and during school, when not practicing for sports, I worked after school and on Saturdays. I received a first-hand education in commerce and how my own family was impacted by all those financial realities. But, I was also now saving more money – and because my parents taught me to, giving more money to the church. Middle schoolers need to learn about family budgets. They need some comprehension of reality, other than the occasional "Do you think money grows on trees?" Did you ever stop to think, if you have not taught them different, maybe they do think it grows on trees. Also, remember, by this age, they are competing with all the other kids at school – clothes, shoes, style – all that stuff is suddenly a big deal in their life. As a parent, it is up to you to coach and teach the values necessary for them to cope. Don't forget, to them it feels like a competition.

High school – the conversation about college should have begun early in their elementary education. The big three in most family budgets are houses, retirement and college. By the time I reached high school I had graduated from the cigar box to a bank account. I even had a checking account. My Dad made certain, unlike my four-year-old daughter, that I knew that there was not an endless supply of money in that account. It contained only what I put in the account and not a penny more. Many teens acquire part-time jobs, just as I did. Some teens are not sure they want to attend college, and are we as parents preparing them to plunge head-long into the adult work-a-day world, and can they be independent enough to survive? In high school I learned about the cost of owning a car – which is much more than the purchase price. I learned about auto insurance and auto maintenance. I knew how the banking system worked. I knew the basics about taxes and Social Security. Why would we not want our teenagers to know all of this long before they leave high school?

Parents, remember, if not you, then who, will provide your children with values and wisdom regarding money?

Widows and more.... Let's begin with some straightforward facts from Bank of America: At some point 80-90% of women will be solely responsible for their financial well-being at some point in their life; Only 48% of women feel confident about their finances; Only 28% of women feel empowered to take action relative to finances. Too often couples find discussions about money uncomfortable and difficult, so those conversations get packed away for another day. Until! In a 2018 Merrill Lynch study 61% of the women in the study said they were willing to talk about their own death, but did not want to broach the subject with their spouse. Yet, there are major trends and significant shifts occurring in American culture that cannot be ignored.

- Life expectancy – women, on average live 15 years longer than their male spouses. Thus, family finances transfer to the wife before it passes on to the next generation.
- Wealth transfers – McKinsey & Company reports that an estimated $59 trillion will be passed from baby boomers to their spouses during the next forty years – and $30 trillion will be controlled by women.
- Divorce – currently it appears that almost half of all marriages will end in divorce, and that is mostly driven by couples over the age of 50, and many are among the most wealthy.

All the data suggest that eight out of ten women will be completely responsible for their financial affairs at some point in their life. We Also know that women own 51.3% of all the wealth in America and control 48% of all the estates worth more than $5 million. That same data states that at some point 95% of women will manage family wealth on their own. All of this points to the urgency for and the need for preparation and planning.

Widowed women outnumber widowed men by a 3:1 ratio, and those women have an average age of 57. I am counted among those men who have been widowed. In my book *Goodnight, Sweetheart* I recount the days, the months and the years of agony and grief in knowing and watching my sweet Judy changed by and taken by Alzheimer's Disease.

In the book I describe grief that comes with such great loss. I also discuss grief counseling, as defined by the counseling and psychological community. I have a degree in counseling, so I agree and support the need for healthy grieving. What I don't think we can do is fit grief into a process, or stages, or anything else. It is, at first, sheer numbness and chaos. I refer to it in the book as a time of reeling, feeling, dealing, and ultimately, some degree of healing. Here is reality....amid the chaos, our financial lives do not stop. There is no grace period. Thus, the more advance preparation one makes, the more navigable the flow of life can become.

These thoughts and suggestions have been useful for others:

- Finances – we have all heard the adage, "Don't make any decisions that are not necessary while you are still processing your loss." I can attest that our thinking can be clouded by the waves of grief that seemingly roll over us for an extended period. However, there are typically a few decisions and actions that cannot be postponed. There could be some immediate expenses relative to funeral expenses that must be addressed. Dealing with life insurance companies can be done anytime, but the sooner one feels confident to do so, this process tends to be relatively simple, and it can quickly become the source of income. Somewhat related to the life insurance, there could also be certain survivor benefits that will require attention. My experience has been that most people handle these simpler affairs thirty to sixty days after their loss. Of course, during these first weeks one should revisit bills, loans and any financial obligations that demand attention.
- Estate Settlement – As discussed earlier in this book, the time to complete a carefully determined estate plan is while in good health and of a sound mind. Assuming that was done, it will be necessary to address certain issues within the first nine months following the death of a spouse. A will is a document that requires Probate (part of the legal system), and in some states, depending on the size of the estate, an

attorney may or may not be required. In the state I reside in an estate greater than $25,000.00 requires an attorney present throughout the process. Some will have prepared a Living Trust, and to the extent that the trust "owns" assets, those assets will pass outside of probate. Also, any accounts, including life insurance, that contain a named beneficiary will pass outside of probate. This estate settlement phase includes removing the name of the deceased from any form of property (real estate, retirement accounts, bank accounts, brokerage accounts, etc). The time to simplify this phase of the process is long before the need occurs.

- Grieve inwardly and outwardly – Good grief involves times of reflection, gratitude, thankfulness, talking with others, praying, meditating...and lots of tears. I also found great help by participating in a group at my church. Our group was blessed to have a Hospice Chaplain facilitate as we worked together through the *Grief Share* materials and process. There is also ample professional help available as needed.
- Keep family and friends close – Personally I tend to turn inward, sort of "circle the wagons," when life gets hard. Frankly, that is not an emotionally healthy way to deal with pain – and losing a spouse brings a lot of pain! Let people in your life, in your thoughts. No, they won't always know what to say. Yes, sometimes they will say the wrong things. But they care and let them love you and show you that they care. Attending the *Grief Share* sessions is what helped me break out the shell I formed around myself. The lyrics to the song *People Need People*, can seem a bit haunting, but its real message is spot on.... *"the weak need the strong, the strong need the weak, we've all got something missing...we're all searching for an answer that's been there all along. People.* Yes, people. Let them in, let them cry with you, let them sit silently with you. Be glad they want to show up for you.
- Welcome support – You don't have to do everything at one time, and you don't have to do anything alone. Don't wait,

reach out to loved ones. Don't tell yourself that you don't want to be a bother or a burden. Hogwash! My Dad raised pigs, and just in case you don't know, that word is another word for swill. Slop! In our vernacular it has come to mean nonsense, ridiculous, a lie. Don't give in to the nonsense that you don't need or deserve help. I am encouraging you to ask for help. Reach out, reach across - be willing to ask for support.

- Stay involved with your church – I know, I know.... we can feel like a third wheel. Our social circle is now missing our spouse, and often others aren't sure how to relate to us. During my wife's extended illness, I often felt cut off from church friends. Usually, it is not that they want to exclude us, they just are not sure how we want to be included and related to. Show them that you want to be included, and you do that by staying involved. Retreating to the confines of your living or bedroom won't lead to anything productive, and it won't bring healing to your heart.

Divorce brings massive changes into our lives on multiple levels, and perhaps none more pronounced than finances. Much of what I have written about the personal and financial issues related to losing a spouse by death is applicable to losing a spouse by divorce. Divorce represents the death of a marriage, and all the hopes and dreams that were equated to that marriage die with it. Like any death, the death of a marriage requires a process of grieving, healing and planning. An initial step could be taking time to self-assess and begin mapping a path toward desired outcomes. What do you want your future life to look like? How will the relationship with a former spouse be dealt with, initially and long term? Complete an inventory of your finances. Include all known costs and plan for the unexpected. What are to be the sources of income? Develop a spending plan (budget). Be precise, be realistic. Include time reviewing all of your insurance coverage – life insurance, health insurance, property & casualty insurance, disability income insurance – and, while doing that update all the beneficiary designations on life insurance and retirement accounts, etc. Maintain and strengthen as many of your relationships as possible – friends, family, church, professional. As a Pastor and Licensed Professional Counselor, I can also attest to the value of spending time with a faith-based counselor. That person will be an amazing resource for you.

We all know that life is filled many uncertainties and contingencies. Within our families we can, and should work together, to ensure that collectively we have done all within our abilities to become financially healthy and prepared individuals and families. Too much is at stake to neglect careful preparation.

CHAPTER 16

The Progress: Creating Accountability for Personal Success

As I sit at my desk and begin this chapter, I have just returned to my study from a visit to a doctor's office. Lately I find myself, half-jokingly, making remarks about how many "ologists" I have in my life these days. A fellow can fill up a calendar rather quickly with the appointments to those "ologists." Why, there is one for my eyes, my ears, my heart, my lungs, my kidneys, my bones, my skin, my brain, and oh yes, let's not forget the one that makes me drink that awful potion that keeps me up all night. I'm not kidding, I am on the radar of each one of those. Sometimes it seems a bit overwhelming. Thankfully, I have Dr. Richard Peters – whose title has changed with the times from General Practitioner to Internal Medicine to Primary Care Physician. Frankly, without him I'm not sure I could keep all those other docs in alignment with my long-term health needs. I need Dr. Peters to help me understand the implications of recommendations, treatment plans, prescribed medicines, potential risks, and the intended outcomes – and even a few unintended consequences. It also just happens that next week I have my annual wellness exam visit to Dr. Peters on my calendar. Whew, and thank goodness. Not only will he use the tools and techniques of his trade to evaluate my current health, but he will take the time to help me evaluate and process what my "ologists" are doing for me. In fact, some of the "ologists" are part of my life because he recommended them. They key is, someone is standing alongside me, helping me make good, well informed decisions about my health.

Now, it seems to me that what I described as my current reality (don't forget, I have been around for more than seven decades) with doctors, is exactly what I did all those years for my financial planning clients. I used my education, available tools and technologies, up-to-date screening and analytic processes, and consultations with other professionals (lawyers, bankers, financial analyst, accountants, investment specific experts) to provide the best possible financial health for my clients. Just as my primary care doctor, along with all those other specialists, provide me with the best opportunity for better physical health, so it is that I firmly believe that my financial planner provides me with the best option for financial success. Yes, you read that correctly. Especially now that I am "retired," I have a personal financial planner. We talk often and meet regularly to ensure that I understand the "financial pulse" of what the economy is doing, and that we do scans and screens to ensure all the moving parts of my financial life remain in harmony. Why bother? For the same reason I see Dr. Peters and the "ologist." I want to live, and when it comes to my money, I want it to live as long as I live (actually the chart says it will not die with me unless I do something really stupid).

So, here's the point. We all need someone to help us track the progress of our financial plans. Someone willing to tell us the truth, jolt us back to reality when needed, to give us insight, affirmation, and correction when needed. I am no more willing to trust the "life of my money" to what I can find on the internet, than I am to trust my physical life to what I can find on the internet. As the subtitle to this chapter suggests, we all must ask for help in creating accountability for our personal financial success. After all, this is too important to leave to chance or the philosophy of "I hope so." My experience has been that if we fail to develop a plan to succeed, the default plan is a plan to fail. We must be intentional with our financial plans if we expect a good outcome. Investment products, that is the form of an investment (Mutual Fund, ETF, Real Estate, Stocks, Bonds, etc) are commodities. Financial planning is not a commodity, rather it is a combination of art and science and relationships, wrapped in the form of one human being interacting with another human being, both of whom can relate on a soul level. No textbook, no computer, no algorithm can do that. Financial planning begins and ends with an actual relationship. Why would we want it any other way?

As Christians we are very familiar with God's perspective on accountability. God knows me (and you) all too well. If not for the matter of accountability in most areas of my life I would be inclined to live a lesser life. If we are honest, we all agree with that statement. As a child of Billy and Iva Johnston, I was accountable to them. In my early work life, I was accountable to my bosses. In college I was accountable to my professors. As a pastor I was accountable to both God and the congregation. As a business owner, I was accountable to my business partner, the regulators, and certainly to the clients. In my marriage I am accountable to my wife. We cannot hide behind the cloak of Christianity and think that we do not have the need for accountability. I have yet to meet the person, whether they admit it or not, who does not need accountability. In the corporate sense accountability is the acceptance of responsibility for honest and ethical behavior toward others. Sadly, in current culture, it is not uncommon for big businesses to lose their bearings, abandon their values – all for the sake of profits. We are currently reaping the whirlwind of a government that knows little about accountability. Even churches can lose their way. But here is what I know… God demands accountability. Romans 14:12 puts it plainly, *"So then each of us will give an account of himself to God."* Every thought, every word, every action, every decision matters to God. My most oft repeated prayer of repentance revolves around attitudes and actions that I know can be hurtful and can even hinder the message of the gospel. I needed repeated reminders that Jesus said, *"For I tell you… people will give an account for every careless word they speak…."* For those who teach and lead other Christians there is added accountability as indicated in Hebrews 13:17, *"…because they keep watch over you as those who must give an account."* And James 3:1 adds *"…you know that we who teach will be judged with greater strictness."* The Apostle Paul cautioned the Corinthians that *"each one's work will become manifest, for the Day will disclose it, …for the fire will test what sort of work each has done."*

Perhaps, for Christians, there is no more dramatic picture of accountability than is found in 2 Corinthians 5:10. Jesus told several parables that illustrate God's point of view about accountability. God clearly demands we be accountable.

So, while I know that God demands accountability, I also know that our own heart (mind) deceives us regarding accountability. The Bible certainly confirms that statement. I recall a book titled, "I'm OK, You're OK." In 1972, the year I graduated from college, it made the New York Times best seller list. The author proposes that we encounter four stages in our life, culminating in the I'm OK, you're OK state of being. I'm not recommending the book, nor am I offering commentary on the book. I am only suggesting that the title does not align with how God views us when we are outside the sphere of an ongoing relationship with Him. Jeremiah 17:9 says, *"The heart is deceitful above all things, and desperately sick; who can understand it?"* Mark's gospel adds commentary for us, *"For from within, out of the heart of man, comes evil thoughts, sexual immorality, theft, murder, adultery, coveting, wickedness, deceit, sensuality, envy, slander, pride, foolishness. All these things come from within, and they defile a person."* The next time you are inclined to tell someone to follow their heart you may want to reconsider. This point means that we cannot trust ourselves to always do the right thing. We cannot believe that we will always hold ourselves accountable. Our best intentions can be derailed.

Yes, God demands accountability. No, because I can deceive myself, I cannot be trusted to always hold myself accountable. There is also the problem of the devil. You see, the devil distorts matters of accountability. The Bible labels the devil as the father of all lies. That alone is enough for me to be concerned about an enemy who delights in ruining lives, maligning reputations and wreaking havoc. Eden's record contains the first distortion of the devil when he convinced Eve that she would not be held accountable for violating a command from God. Look around, do you see paradise? Nope! When we fall for the distorted truth offered by the devil, we can expect similar results. And don't miss God's question, *"What have you done?'*

Therefore, my own inability to always hold myself accountable, combined with the devil's constant attempts to distort the truth and

God's reputation as requiring accountability in all matters, then it holds that my future success – including my financial future – will demand that I create partnerships with others to hold me accountable. In other words, it's all about ownership of your future. Its success or failure rests with you.

How do we create an accountability partnership? Many churches offer groups, such as Crown Financial and Financial Peace University, or similar small groups. My experience with these groups has been positive. I have facilitated both formats that I mentioned, and I found that the majority of those involved, both couples and singles, took their involvement seriously and reaped the rewards of the knowledge they acquired and the disciplines they developed. There is a wealth of printed material that can assist you, but I highly recommend that you find that person or persons that you can meet with on a periodic basis to share information and ideas. There are fee-based financial planners that you can retain to meet with you once or twice a year to ensure that your plan remains sound, and that you are indeed on target to reach your financial goals. In a previous chapter we discussed setting SMART goals. Once those are determined and methods of implementation are settled on, it then becomes a matter of staying the course and celebrating the successes. So, yes, I believe most people need a coach, a guide to provide direction and to make corrections as needed. But ultimately, it's your discipline and determination that will lead to success. So, what is your SMART plan for becoming financially independent?

Afterword
FREE AT LAST

As you have probably determined by now, there is no easy way to reach financial freedom. If you were looking for an easy way out, some simple formula, my word to you is, "It does not exist." Yes, there are some simple concepts, some basic guidelines, but they require commitment and discipline from you in following the principles set forth in this book. I have sought diligently to present the truth regarding money and life management. Jesus said that the truth is liberating, and my prayer for each reader of this book is that you will discover new hope and freedom in your exercise of these principles.

Every journey begins with the first step. Your faith journey to financial freedom is no different, it too begins with a step. I challenge you to "roll up your sleeves" and prayerfully take the necessary steps to gain the desired freedom.

Freedom...peace of mind...security...a sense of well-being...a feeling of accomplishment...a sense of direction in your life; all of this and more awaits you! **Free at last! Free at last!** The sweet shout of a captive set free; that's you and me as we meet on the pathway that leads to financial freedom.

Dictionary Of Financial Planning Terms

ACTUARY - the science of using mathematical statistics and probability to manage and mitigate financial risk and uncertainty.

ACCREDITED ESTATE PLANNER (AEP) - a graduate level specialization in estate planning.

ANNUITY- A contract between an insurance company and an individual in which the company agrees to provide an income, fixed or variable in amount, for a specified period in exchange for a stipulated amount of money.

ASSETS - Anything owned that has monetary value.

BEAR MARKET- A bear market is one that is sharply declining because investors believe that stock prices, or the market as a whole, will fall.

BENEFICIARY - The person designated to receive the proceeds or benefits accruing under a life insurance policy or an annuity; also, the person who is to receive the benefits of a trust estate. A beneficiary can be an individual, a company, an organization, etc.

BID AND ASKED - A "bid" price is the highest price that someone is willing to pay for a stock. The "asked" price, on the other hand, is the lowest price at which someone is willing to sell.

BLUE CHIP - A common stock that is highly esteemed as an investment based on the following criteria: Earnings in good times and

DICTIONARY OF FINANCIAL PLANNING TERMS

bad over a long period time; 25 years or more of paying quarterly cash dividends; leadership in solid, established industries coupled with solid expectations for continued success.

BULL MARKET - A bull market is one that is sharply advancing because investors believe that stock prices, or the market as a whole, will rise.

CAPITAL GAINS - Gain realized through the sale or exchange of a capital asset, property owned for investment, such as securities and real estate.

CAPITAL LOSSES - Losses incurred through the sale or exchange of capital assets.

CASH SURRENDER VALUE - Before the maturity of your life insurance policy, or before death, you can cash in the policy and receive an amount of money called the cash surrender value.

CERTIFICATE OF DEPOSIT - Also a CD. A certificate for a time deposit earning a specified rate of interest over a given time.

CERTIFIED FINANCIAL PLANNER (CFP®) - a type of financial advisor who possesses of the most rigorous certifications in the financial industry. They assess the financial needs of individuals and help them with decisions on investments, tax laws, insurance and estate planning.

CHARTERED FINANCIAL CONSULTANT (ChFC) - a financial consultant who has completed rigorous and comprehensive training in financial education. In addition to the typical financial planning courses the ChFC requirements include the study of Employee Benefits Planning, Asset Protection Planning applications of comprehensive financial planning and consulting.

COMMON STOCK - Securities that represent ownership interest in a corporation.

CREDIT LIFE INSURANCE - Term life insurance which pays off a loan if the borrower dies. This is sometimes required by lenders.

CUMULATIVE PREFERRED STOCK - A stock with the provision that if one or more of its dividends are omitted, these arrears must be paid before dividends are paid on the common stock.

DISABILITY INCOME INSURANCE - A type of insurance that pays benefits while a person is disabled due to injury or illness.

DICTIONARY OF FINANCIAL PLANNING TERMS

DOLLAR COST AVERAGING - the systematic movement of money as a strategy with the goal of reducing the impact of volatility on the purchase of financial assets.

EQUITY - The value of a person's ownership in real property or investment securities. For example, current market value of your home, less principle remaining on the mortgage, in your equity in that home.

EQUITY ASSETS - Investments that represent ownership interest (as opposed to a debt obligation) such as stocks, real estate, commodities, and limited partnerships.

ESTATE TAXES - Taxes imposed by the federal government (and by some state governments) on the taxable estate of a person who has died.

EXCHANGE TRADED FUND - A pooled type of investment, similar to a mutual fund. An ETF typically tracks a particular index, sector, commodity or other assets. An ETF is a basket of securities that trade on an exchange just as a stock would trade.

FACE AMOUNT - This is the amount of death benefit as stated on the face of an insurance policy. This is the amount of a policy that is paid at death or at contract maturity, less any policy loans or withdrawals are made.

FIDUCIARY - a person with a fiduciary duty is called a fiduciary. Being a fiduciary means that the person must always act in a way that will benefit the persons (clients) they represent.

FINRA - Financial Industry Regulatory Authority - FINRA enables investors and firms to participate in the market with confidence by safeguarding its integrity by regulating brokerage firms and exchange markets.

GIFT TAXES - Taxes imposed by the federal government upon an individual's lifetime transfers of money or property by gift.

GOVERNMENT OBLIGATIONS - Instruments of the U.S. government public debt. Examples are Treasury bills, notes, bonds, and savings bonds. These are fully backed by the U.S. government.

GROUP LIFE INSURANCE - Employers or unions offer insurance to their employees or members on a group basis. This often results in lower cost premiums and no medical examination.

HR-10 RETIREMENT PLAN (KEOGH) - A tax-favored

retirement plan which may be established by an individual who has earned income from self-employment. Contributions made to the plan are deductible from the self-employed's income. This type of plan also provides retirement security for employees working for the self-employed individual. The plan can take the form of a defined benefit plan, a money purchase plan or a defined contribution plan.

INHERITANCE TAXES - Taxes imposed by some states upon the passing of property of a deceased person's estate to their heirs. It is a tax upon the heir's right to receive his share of the estate.

INVESTMENT - The allocation of money or resources to gain additional resources, often through capital appreciation or interest income.

IRA - An Individual Retirement Account, a tax-favored retirement plan which can be established by any individual with earned income in a calendar year. Current 2023 contribution limits are $6,500 for an individual, or $7,500 for individuals over age 50. The amount contributed to an IRA is typically not subject to federal income taxes in the year of the contribution and all of its earnings accumulate on a tax-deferred basis until withdrawn.

JOINT and SURVIVOR - An arrangement under which the owner of the annuity elects to have payments contribute to another person for that person's lifetime, after the original annuitant's death.

JOINT TENANCY - Form of co-ownership which refers to a jointly held property. While all joint tenants are alive, each one has an individual interest in the whole property. When one joint tenant dies, his or her interest passes to the surviving joint tenant or tenants. The last surviving joint tenant obtains the entire joint property.

KINGDOM ADVISORS - an organization which equips and empowers its members to carry biblical financial wisdom to their clients, peers and community.

LEVEL PREMIUM INSURANCE - This is a type of insurance where the yearly premium is the same over the life of the policy.

LIABILITIES - All debts and other obligations owed to creditors.

LIMITED PARTNERSHIP - A form of business consisting of one or more general partners who manage the partnership's investments and a group of limited partners who invest the capital. The partnership itself pays no taxes. Instead, partners report their pro rata share of partnership profits, losses, and deductions on their own individual tax returns.

MANAGED ACCOUNT - an investment vehicle where a professional manager oversees a pool of assets at the plan level. It can provide a way for an individual investor to benefit from a private investment managers professional expertise.

MARGIN - A partial payment on investment units, the remainder of which is loans by the trader. Investors who buy on margin hope the price will go up fast enough to cover their loan, and thereby increase their buying power. If prices drop, however, they will also increase their losses.

MONEY MARKET FUND - A mutual fund that specializes in investing in short-term securities.

MORTGAGE - A lien of property created by a pledge of that property as security for repayment of a loan. It provides for the transfer of the property to the lender if the borrower defaults.

MUNICIPAL BONDS - The obligations of states, cities, towns, school districts, and public authorities. In general, interest paid on municipal bonds is exempt from federal taxes and possibly from state and local taxes, too.

OPTIONS - a contract that gives you the right to buy or sell a financial product at an agreed upon price for a specific period.

PASSIVE INCOME OR LOSSES - Income or losses from investments in a business or trade in which the investor does not actively and substantially participate in the business. Examples include limited partnerships and owning certain types of rental income property.

PENSION - Regular income paid to a worker after retirement. In many instances, survivors receive this income after the worker dies.

PERMANENT LIFE INSURANCE - Also whole life insurance. Any type of life insurance, other than term, which has the following characteristics: A cash value that can be borrowed, used as collateral, or withdrawn by surrendering the policy; and a lump-sum benefit payable at death.

PERSONAL FINANCIAL PLANNER - One who helps

DICTIONARY OF FINANCIAL PLANNING TERMS

individuals in an ongoing process to arrange and coordinate their personal and financial affairs to enable them to achieve their objectives.

PERSONAL PROPERTY - Generally, any property other than real estate.

PORTFOLIO - All assets held by a mutual fund at any specific time, and thus, held by the shareholders. Or total investments held by an individual.

PREFERRED STOCK - A class of stock with a claim on the company's earnings before payment may be made on the common stock if the company liquidates or declares a dividend.

PRINCIPAL - The amount of money that is financed, borrowed, or invested.

PROCEEDS - The amount payable under a life insurance policy upon the death of the insured. The proceeds consist of the face amount of the contract, plus accumulated dividends (if any), plus whatever amounts may be payable on riders, less any money owed to the life insurance company on the policy in the form of loans and interest on those loans.

PROBATE - The process of proving that the written will of the deceased is valid.

REGISTERED REPRESENTATIVE - a person engaged in the solicitation or handling of accounts or orders for the purchase or sale of securities for the accounts of customers of the advisory or brokerage firm.

REGISTERED INVESTMENT ADVISOR - an individual financial advisor or company that provides clients with financial advice. RIA's have a fiduciary duty to act in the best interest of the clients. Other persons who sell financial products may not be held to the fiduciary standard and may only have to offer advice that meets suitability standards.

SECURITY - An investment of money in a common enterprise with the expectation of profit from the effort of others. A stock, bond, limited partnership, or similar investment.

STOCK OPTION - Companies often provide the opportunity for their key employees to buy stock in the company at favorable prices and terms. This is called a stock option.

SUITABILITY - this standard requires brokers and investment advisors to recommend investments that are suitable for the client. This is not the same as the fiduciary standard where the fiduciary is required to place their client's best interests first.

TAX-EXEMPT - Certain kinds of income not subject to federal income tax. Included is income from most state and municipal bonds and most Social Security payments (for taxpayers up to certain income limits).

TAX-EXEMPT INTEREST - The interest earned on tax-exempt securities is not includable in a shareholder's gross income for Federal income tax purposes. In most states, the income from municipal bonds issued within a state is tax-exempt to residents of that state.

TAX-SHELTER - In some instances, a device whereby a taxpayer may reinvest earnings on capital without paying current income tax on them. Examples include company and individual pension plans, contributions to which are not considered income until they are paid out, and life insurance policies, where the interest earned on each policy is allowed to accrue without being considered taxable income.

TENANCY IN COMMON - A form of co-ownership. Upon the death of a co-owner, his or her interest passes to his or her estate and not surviving owner or owners.

TERM LIFE INSURANCE - This type of insurance covers a limited specific period of time. In the event of death, benefits will be paid only if death occurs during the period the policy is in force.

TREASURY BOND - A U.S. government long-term security sold to the public with a maturity greater than five years.

TREASURY STOCK - A stock issued by a company but later reacquired. It may be held in the company's treasury indefinitely, reissued to the public or retired. Treasury stock receives no dividends and has no vote while held by the company.

TRUST - A legal arrangement by which title to property is given to one party who manages it for the benefit of the beneficiaries of the trust.

TRUSTEE - An individual or corporation appointed or required by law to administer or execute the trust for the beneficiaries of the trust.

UNIT INVESTMENT TRUST - A limited portfolio of bonds or

other securities in which investors may purchase shares. It differs from a mutual fund in that no new securities will be added to the portfolio and the trust terminates at a specified future date.

UNIVERSAL LIFE INSURANCE - This type of insurance combines pure insurance protection with a savings element that accumulates tax deferred at current interest rates. The premium amount and payment schedule are flexible and the policyowner can increase or decrease his/her coverage without purchasing a new policy.

VARIABLE LIFE INSURANCE - This type of insurance combines pure insurance protection with a savings element that can be invested in a variety of asset portfolios. Earnings on the savings element accumulate tax deferred and the policyowner can transfer funds among asset portfolios with varying investment objectives.

WILL - A legal declaration of a person's wishes concerning the disposition of his property after his death, the guardianship of his children, and the administration of his estate.

YIELD - Also known as return. The dividends or interest paid by a company expressed as a percentage of the current price or, if you own the security, it's original price. The return on a stock is figured by dividing the total of dividends paid in the preceding 12 months by the current price or, if you are the owner, the original price.

Appendix

The Four Cornerstones of Financial Balance

1 Cash Reserves

Money available for immediate needs or emergency use.

Examples:
- Passbook savings
- Money market funds
- Short-term certificates of deposit

Protection 2

Money for those unforeseen events that can threaten your family's financial well-being.

Examples:
- Health, casualty, disability, and life insurance

3 Fixed Assets

Money set aside or invested at fixed rates of return, usually for specific lengths of time, to provide income and a predictable rate of growth.

Examples:
- Corporate and municipal bonds and bond funds
- Some unit investment trusts
- Investment and savings certificates
- Cash value annuities
- Cash value life insurance

Equity Assets 4

Money invested in enterprises whose value and rate of return may vary.

Examples:
- Real estate
- Common stocks
- Equity mutual funds
- Variable annuities
- Commodities

Document Locator

This list of important documents and people will assist you and your family in identifying information and those people pertinent to your long-term plans.

Estate Documents

1. _____
2. _____
3. _____
4. _____
5. _____

Life Insurance Documents

1. _____
2. _____
3. _____
4. _____
5. _____
6. _____

Health & Long-Term Care Insurance

1. _____
2. _____
3. _____
4. _____
5. _____
6. _____
7. _____
8. _____

Disability Insurance Documents

1. _____
2. _____
3. _____
4. _____

Automobile & Homeowners Insurance

1. _____
2. _____
3. _____
4. _____
5. _____

Banks & Financial Institutions

1. _____
2. _____
3. _____
4. _____
5. _____
6. _____
7. _____
8. _____

Investment Accounts

1. _____
2. _____
3. _____
4. _____
5. _____
6. _____
7. _____
8. _____

Retirement Accounts

1. _____
2. _____
3. _____
4. _____
5. _____
6. _____
7. _____
8. _____

Funeral Instructions

1. _____
2. _____
3. _____
4. _____
5. _____
6. _____

General Financial Notes

_____
_____
_____
_____
_____
_____
_____

Key People

- Minister: _____
- Funeral Director: _____
- Financial Advisor: _____
- Attorney: _____
- Banker: _____
- Physician: _____
- Personal contacts: _____

"Six Basic Needs" Worksheet

Most financial advisors agree that there are six basic needs that should be addressed in any well-designed financial plan. These six basic needs are listed below in column A. Look at each need; then, in column B, make a note of what you are doing now to address that need.

Now look back at the previous page. Each scale corresponds with one of the basic needs. Transcribe your rating from the previous page onto column C of this page. Look at how important you rated each of the needs; then look at what you are doing now. Based upon the importance of each need to you, use the last column to show how adequate you feel your current activities are.

(A) Six Basic Needs	(B) Here is What I'm Doing Now	(C) Value Rating From Previous Page	(D) Do I Feel This Is Adequate?
1. Income for Retirement			☐ Yes ☐ No ☐ Don't Know
2. Minimizing Taxes			☐ Yes ☐ No ☐ Don't Know
3. Emergency Money			☐ Yes ☐ No ☐ Don't Know
4. Protection			☐ Yes ☐ No ☐ Don't Know
5. Education			☐ Yes ☐ No ☐ Don't Know
6. Capital Accumulation			☐ Yes ☐ No ☐ Don't Know

Financial Planning Flow Chart

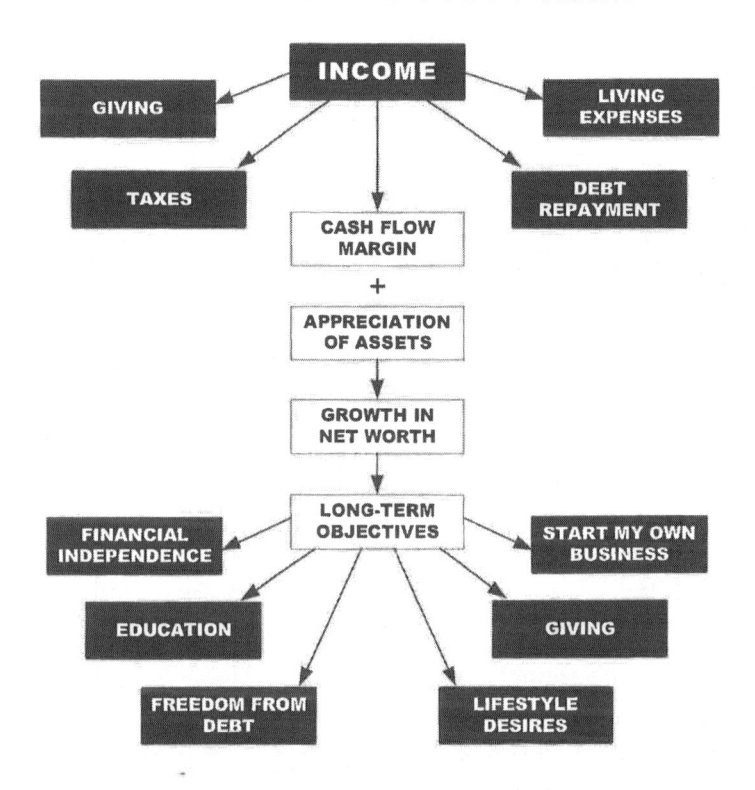

```
                        INCOME
        ┌──────────────┬──┬──────────────┐
     GIVING                           LIVING EXPENSES
     TAXES                            DEBT REPAYMENT
                        ↓
                  CASH FLOW MARGIN
                        +
                  APPRECIATION OF ASSETS
                        ↓
                  GROWTH IN NET WORTH
                        ↓
                  LONG-TERM OBJECTIVES
   ┌────────────┬───────┼───────┬────────────┐
FINANCIAL   EDUCATION  FREEDOM  LIFESTYLE  GIVING   START MY OWN
INDEPENDENCE           FROM DEBT DESIRES             BUSINESS
```

CAPITAL ACCUMULATION GOALS

This area of financial planning involves setting some priorities on your savings and investment plans. First, for what purpose are you accumulating money? Perhaps for a new home, an automobile, education, retirement, cash reserves....or any other goal that is of value to you.

For each goal there are a few key questions and considerations:

- Where am I now financially?
- How much money will I need to meet my objective?
- How much time do I have?
- What steps must I take to achieve my objective?

Obviously, some of our thinking will focus on the short-term decisions and actions that I need to take, while others focus on the long-term. What should you consider, that will impact the next six months? Are there any potential financial pitfalls on the horizon? What financial fears creep in? Are you making progress toward your goals? Are you over-extended? Are your debts hindering your progress?

Now it's time to put to paper those financial goals and aspirations. Remember, we need SMART goals. Our goals need to be specific, measurable, actionable, realistic and time bound. To ensure we do not easily discourage ourselves, goals should be both realistic and challenging.

For each goal we need to develop key parameters: (step 1) identify any barriers that exist, (2) Set a time limit, a deadline, for accomplishing the goal, (3) establish an accountability system, (4) list other important concerns and considerations. Repeat this process for each financial goal:

Goal: _____

Step 1: _____

Step 2: _____

Step 3: _____

Step 4: _____

_____

_____

Your risk tolerance for your financial goals

Your tolerance for assuming risk is one of the most important aspects of planning to achieve your financial goals. It refers to the degree to which you are willing to invest, recognizing the possibility that an investment may lose value or yield less than its anticipated return. We'll use this information to make plan recommendations based on your goals and time frame. As you take action on your plan, we'll also look at the risk level within each of your accounts, as your risk tolerance may vary based on your specific goals and expectations for each unique account.

Risk tolerance category	Description
Conservative	I am willing to accept the lowest return potential in exchange for the lowest potential fluctuation in my account value even if it may not keep pace with inflation.
Moderately conservative	I am willing to accept a relatively low return potential in exchange for relatively low fluctuation in account value.
Moderate	I am willing to accept a moderate return potential in exchange for some fluctuation in account value.
Moderately aggressive	I am seeking a relatively high return potential and am willing to accept a relatively high fluctuation and potentially substantial loss in my account value.
Aggressive	I am seeking the highest return potential and am willing to accept the highest fluctuation and could lose most or all of my account value.

Risk tolerance for <client first>
Risk tolerance for client
Category _____

If you were to lean toward one category, which would it be — more conservative or more aggressive?
_____

Risk tolerance for <co-client first>
Risk tolerance for co-client
Category _____

If you were to lean toward one category, which would it be — more conservative or more aggressive?
_____

Risk tolerance for joint goals
Risk tolerance for joint goals
(if applicable)
Category _____

If you were to lean toward one category, which would it be — more conservative or more aggressive?
_____

List any goals for which your risk tolerance may be different than noted above (e.g., short-term goals such as funding education, saving for a large purchase, establishing an emergency fund).
_____
_____

How Much Will I Need?

Planning for Retirement Income

Current annual household income (after taxes)	$ _____ (A)
Current annual household expenses	_____ (B)
80% of B =	_____ (C)
Your current age _____ (D)	
Your current life expectancy (see table below)	_____ (E)
Expected retirement age	_____ (F)
Subtract F from E (= number of years of expected retirement)	_____ (G)
Average amount needed for retirement (today's dollars) G x C =	_____ (H)

Life Expectancy Table*

Male smoker	Male nonsmoker	Current age	Female smoker	Female nonsmoker
26.6	31.2	45	31.9	34.4
22.5	26.7	50	27.6	30.0
18.7	22.4	55	23.6	25.7
15.2	18.4	60	19.8	21.5
12.1	14.7	65	16.1	17.5
9.5	11.4	70	12.7	13.8
7.3	8.6	75	9.6	10.4
5.5	6.3	80	7.1	7.5
4.2	4.5	85	5.0	5.2
3.1	3.2	90	3.4	3.5
1.9	1.9	95	1.9	1.9
.5	.5	100	.5	.5

*Source: Principal Mortality Tables; Tillingast, Nelson & Warren, Inc.,

HOW TO CALCULATE ESTIMATED FOUR-YEAR COLLEGE COSTS

If you want to start saving regularly for your child's education, the following steps will help you estimate the amount that you will need to set aside. Tables 1 and 2 will be used in making your calculations.

TABLE 1

Years to Start of college	\	Inflation Factor	\	\
\	4%	6%	8%	10%
1	1.04	1.06	1.08	1.10
2	1.08	1.12	1.17	1.21
3	1.12	1.19	1.26	1.33
4	1.17	1.26	1.36	1.45
5	1.22	1.34	1.47	1.61
6	1.27	1.42	1.59	1.77
7	1.32	1.50	1.71	1.95
8	1.37	1.59	1.85	2.14
9	1.42	1.69	2.00	2.36
10	1.48	1.79	2.16	2.59
11	1.54	1.90	2.33	2.85
12	1.60	2.01	2.52	3.14
13	1.67	2.13	2.72	3.45
14	1.73	2.26	2.94	3.80
15	1.80	2.40	3.17	4.18
16	1.87	2.54	3.43	4.59
17	1.95	2.69	3.70	5.05
18	2.03	2.85	4.00	5.56

TABLE 2

Years to Start of college	Investment Return, After Taxes Of:	\	\
\	4%	6%	8%
1	.981	.971	.962
2	.481	.471	.463
3	.314	.305	.296
4	.231	.222	.213
5	.181	.172	.164
6	.148	.139	.131
7	.124	.116	.108
8	.106	.098	.090
9	.093	.085	.077
10	.082	.074	.066
11	.073	.065	.058
12	.065	.058	.051
13	.059	.051	.045
14	.054	.046	.040
15	.049	.042	.035
16	.045	.038	.032
17	.041	.034	.029
18	.038	.031	.026

COLLEGE COSTS WORK SHEET

Step 1.

Your child's age _____

Step 2.

Enter the number of years until your child begins college. _____

Step 3.

Enter the current annual cost of college. $_____

Step 4.

Multiply this by an inflation factor selected from Table 1. _____

Step 5.

This equals your child's future annual college cost. $_____

Step 6.

Multiply this by 2 for a two-year college or by 4 for four-year college. _____

Step 7.

Your child's estimated future college cost. $_____

Step 8.

Select from Table 2 the investment factor for the investment return that you expect to achieve after taxes. _____

Step 9.

Multiply the estimated cost in Step 7 by the investment factor in Step 8. This is the amount of money that you need to put aside regularly each year to fund your child's education. Divide this amount by 12 to obtain the monthly figure, and by 52 to obtain the weekly figure.

Yearly savings = $_____

Monthly savings = $_____

Weekly savings = $_____

About the Author

Though a native of Alabama, Alan has lived in Chattanooga, Tennessee for more than forty years. He grew up in the rural community of Elmore, near Wetumpka, Alabama. Following graduation from Wetumpka High School he moved to Birmingham, Alabama to begin his educational and career pursuits.

He is both an ordained minister and a Certified Financial Planner (CFP©). His ministry now spans more than fifty years, and he has more than thirty-five years of experience as a financial planner. He has served as Senior Pastor of churches in Alabama and Tennessee and was a founding partner of Oracle Wealth Management (a branch of Ameriprise Financial) in Chattanooga, Tennessee. For the past 35 years Alan has also served as a Teaching Pastor for Abba's House (Central Baptist Church) in Chattanooga.

Alan is also the founder and leader of Path2truth Ministry. He continues to preach and teach and some of that ministry is available on the ministry website as well as Youtube. Path2truth has as its mission "to teach and preach the good news of Jesus Christ – in so doing, to bring Christians into a fresh encounter with God, to equip and encourage the church to be authentic, and to empower believers to share God's redemptive message."

Alan earned his BA degree from the University of Mobile and

additionally holds five advanced degrees and three professional certifications. Those degrees and certifications cover such disciplines as History, Theology, Counseling, Finance and Conflict Management. His educational pursuits spanned Samford University, the University of Mobile, Luther Rice Seminary, UT-Chattanooga, The American College and The University of Alabama.

Among his other books Alan has also written ***Goodnight, Sweetheart – a story of faith, hope & love*** (winner of the SCWC book of the year award 2022) and ***Chosen – answering the call of Jesus.***

Alan is an avid reader and writer, and is as well, an avid fan of college football and basketball. As time permits, he enjoys playing golf.

Most important of all…Alan is a husband to Dowdy, a father to Joy and Jennifer and "G"-daddy to grandchildren Ollie, Maggie, Alex and Benjamin.

Also by Alan Johnston
AVAILABLE FROM AMAZON.COM

Goodnight, Sweetheart – A Story of Faith, Hope & Love (winner of the SCWC book of the year award 2022)

Chosen – Answering the Call of Jesus

Made in the USA
Columbia, SC
18 September 2023